EASY CHRISTMAS PROJECTS you can paint

By Sugar Brushes,

Margaret Wilson & Robyn Thomas

NORTH LIGHT BOOKS
CINCINNATI, OHIO
www.artistsnetwork.com

Dedications

I dedicate this book to my husband, Ronnie. He is always supportive, helpful and painstakingly honest. And to my painting friends, the Tuesday Bunch—Patti, Jeanne, Betty and Madelyn. May we continue to meet, paint, chat and enjoy our friendship with one another.

—MARGARET WILSON

I would like to dedicate this book to my husband, Michael, and our four children: Brandon, Adam, Meghan and Sarah. Without their total support, my traveling and teaching would not be possible. Also to my mom and sister. The two of you own one of everything I have ever painted. Thank you for always believing in me.

—ROBYN THOMAS

 Published by North Light Books, an imprint of F&W Publications, Inc., 4700 East Galbraith Road, Cincinnati, Ohio 45236. (800) 289-0963. First Edition.

Other fine North Light Books are available from your local bookstore, art supply store or direct from the publisher.

06 05 04 03 02   5 4 3 2 1

Library of Congress Cataloging-in-Publication Data

Wilson, Margaret
Easy Christmas projects you can paint/ by Margaret Wilson & Robyn Thomas.
p. cm.
ISBN 1-58180-237-4 (alk. paper)
1. Christmas decorations. 2. Painting. I. Thomas, Robyn- II. Title.

TT900.C4 W555 2002
745.594'12--dc21

EDITOR: Catherine Cochran
DESIGNER: Stephanie Strang
PRODUCTION ARTIST: Cheryl VanDeMotter
PRODUCTION COORDINATOR: Sara Dumford
PHOTOGRAPHERS: Christine Polomsky and Tim Grondin

2001044700

metric conversion chart

TO CONVERT	TO	MULTIPLY BY
Inches	Centimeters	2.54
Centimeters	Inches	0.4
Feet	Centimeters	30.5
Centimeters	Feet	0.03
Yards	Meters	0.9
Meters	Yards	1.1
Sq. Inches	Sq. Centimeters	6.45
Sq. Centimeters	Sq. Inches	0.16
Sq. Feet	Sq. Meters	0.09
Sq. Meters	Sq. Feet	10.8
Sq. Yards	Sq. Meters	0.8
Sq. Meters	Sq. Yards	1.2
Pounds	Kilograms	0.45
Kilograms	Pounds	2.2
Ounces	Grams	28.4
Grams	Ounces	0.04

ABOUT THE AUTHORS

Sugar Brushes

MARGARET WILSON began painting after signing up for a course at a local craft store and has continued ever since. After retiring from teaching, she and her husband moved to Michigan, where she helped organize the Michigan Grapevine Decorative Artist chapter of Society of Decorative Painters. Through this chapter, she met Robyn Thomas and they formed the Sugar Brushes. Currently, she lives in Michigan and enjoys painting and teaching classes.

ROBYN THOMAS began her career by selling children's clothing and stuffed toys at local craft shows. She then collaborated with her husband in making wooden toys. After she had four children, she decided to sign up for a decorative painting class and soon joined the local chapter of Decorative Painters. She met Margaret Wilson and formed the Sugar Brushes. The two travel the country, attend conventions and teach classes.

Acknowledgments

First and foremost we would like to thank our good friends Judy Diephouse and Lynne Deptula. These two ladies have been our mentors from the beginning. They have encouraged, critiqued and played practical jokes on us. Their support has been incredible. Without them, this book would not have been possible.

We also want to thank Catherine Cochran and Christine Polomsky from North Light Books. These two wonderful ladies took away the anxieties we had in making this book. And to all the great people at North Light, we thank you for being so helpful in making our dream to write a book a reality.

TABLE OF CONTENTS

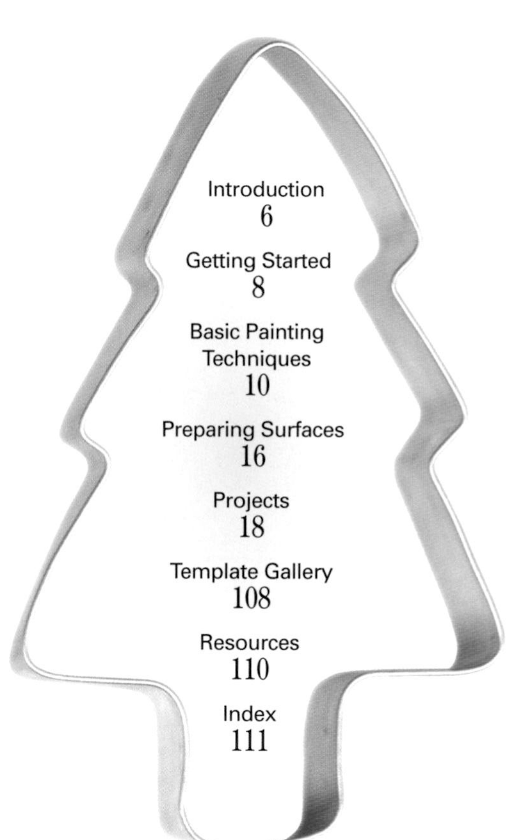

Introduction
6

Getting Started
8

Basic Painting Techniques
10

Preparing Surfaces
16

Projects
18

Template Gallery
108

Resources
110

Index
111

Santa Candle 20

Peppermint Stick Candy Jar 26

Santa Moon Saucer 32

Little Helper's Apron 38

Gingerbread Man Potholder 47

Gossamer Winged Angel 48

Noel Plaque 56

Gingerbread Boy Ornament 64

Snow Day Pot 68

Treetop Santa 78

Snowman and Snowlady Tin 84

Joy Tray 92

Christmas Tree Card Holder 100

INTRODUCTION

Welcome to our book.

Tucked inside of these pages, you will find some delightful projects that will help spread Christmas cheer. Whether you are painting for the family, a special friend, a holiday craft show or yourself, we feel confident that you will find the perfect project in this book. You may want to consider the Treetop Santa to be done as a family project and then save it for the years to come. Or, for that special child, the Little Helper's Apron and Gingerbread Man Potholder will come in handy when making Christmas cookies. If you need to make a quick and easy gift, the adorable gingerbread ornament is a wonderful stocking stuffer. There is something for everyone on your Christmas list.

Don't worry if you have never picked up a brush before. In this book we will teach you basic painting techniques. We will also show you the proper way to prepare surfaces, so you will be able to paint on a variety of mediums—glass, fabric, candle, wood and metal. You will amaze yourself when you complete these festive projects!

Christmastime is the season for giving, and this is your opportunity to share your talents with your friends and family. We hope that you enjoy the painting as much as we enjoyed bringing it to you.

GETTING STARTED

Before you start a project, make sure you have all of the necessary materials. These two pages show you what you need from brushes to paint and primers. You can find all of these supplies at your nearby craft store, and in no time you will have adorable Christmas decorations and gifts.

★Brushes

Brushes pictured left to right: glaze, flat, angle, round, liner, filbert, deerfoot, scrubber, sable, Bobbi's Blender, comb and fan. Sponge brush not pictured.

Brushes are the most important piece of equipment used by craft painters. There are many brands of synthetic brushes on the market, so choose the brand that works best for you. In this book we have used a variety of Royal & Langnickle brushes. A beginner needs a minimum of three basic brushes: a flat or angle, a round and a liner. As you continue to paint, you will find that adding specialty brushes will make the painting go much more quickly. Eventually, you will develop a certain "feel" to achieve a particular look. This feel will help you choose the appropriate brush. As you begin to paint the various projects in the book, please note the types of brushes that we recommend.

Glaze Brush: a soft bristle brush used to finish pieces with varnish or glaze.
Flat Brush: a staple item for craft painters and decorative artists. It is used for basecoating as well as floating color.
Angle Brush: a brush with bristles cut on an angle. It helps the beginner with floating color.
Round Brush: a necessary brush used for basic strokes, daisy petals or leaves.
Liner: an essential brush available in many sizes and lengths. A rule of thumb concerning liners is that the longer the bristles, the less the control. A medium length liner is excellent for our projects.
Filbert Brush: a brush with bristles rounded at the corners so that it looks like an upside-down *U*. This brush is great for making stroke leaves, flower petals or anything that has a rounded edge.
Deerfoot Brush: a round brush that is cut on an angle. It is usually used for stippling, and can also be used for foliage or if you want to achieve a scruffy look.
Scrubber Brush: a round fabric brush with stiff, white nylon bristles.
Sable Brush: a round brush made of natural hairs. It is great for stippling.
Bobbi's Blender: a specialty mop brush with synthetic fibers for acrylic paint. It is excellent for softening lines or fuzzy stippling. It is used best when it is dry and the surface is wet.
Comb Brush: (also called a Rake Brush) a brush commonly used to make fine lines for hair or fur. The bristles are cut at various lengths so that a variety of fine lines are produced simultaneously.
Fan Brush: a brush used in our projects for spattering. The fan brush can help control the direction and the amount of spatter.
Sponge Brush: (not pictured) a brush used to basecoat large surfaces in these projects.

★Additional Supplies

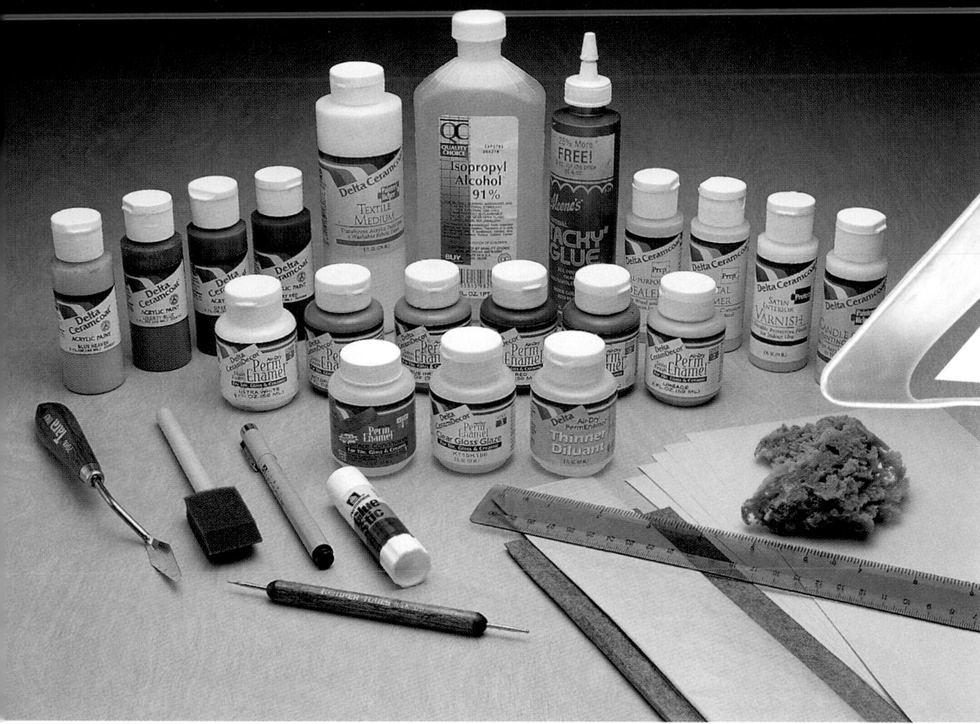

miscellaneous supplies

★

The following are miscellaneous supplies that are required for specific projects

★

Micron .03 permanent pen • clear ruler • cardboard • wax paper • frosted glass finish • scissors • craft glue • glue stick • sail needle • rubbing alcohol • soft cloths

In addition to brushes, you will need the following supplies and tools to create these festive Christmas projects.

Acrylic Paint is a water-based paint. There are a variety of brands of acrylic paints available at craft stores. We used Delta Ceramcoat Acrylic Paint for most of the projects in this book.

Air-Dry Enamel Paint is a group of specialty paints for nonporous surfaces, such as tile, glass and ceramics. We used Delta CeramDecor Air-Dry PermEnamels. They come in a variety of colors. Do not use enamel paints in the same project with acrylic paints.

All-Purpose Sealer is a sealer that prepares wood and other porous surfaces for painting. It allows the paint to go on smoother with fewer coats. It may raise the grain of the wood. If so, a light sanding may be necessary.

Candle and Soap Painting Medium is a medium used with acrylic paint to allow the paint to adhere to a slick surface, such as candles or soap. When using, follow the manufacturer's instructions printed on the bottle.

Clear Gloss Glaze is a glaze used to seal air-dry enamel paint. It acts as a varnish.

Graphite Paper is a paper used to transfer the pattern onto the painting surface. When transferring a pattern to a dark surface, use light or white graphite. When transferring a pattern to a light surface, use dark or black graphite. Your background color will determine which color should be used.

Metal Primer is an undercoat that primes and conditions metals. Follow directions on the bottle before preparing the surface.

Palette Knife is a knife with a flexible steel blade used to mix paint. In this book, it is also used for spattering.

Palette Paper is a basic waxed palette paper designed for acrylic paints. It is inexpensive and disposable.

Sandpaper is a rough paper used to prepare wood for painting. A fine grade of sandpaper will do. We recommend the sanding pads that are available at arts and crafts stores.

Sea Sponge is a natural sponge with various-sized holes. It is used to add dimension and texture when painting.

Stylus is an instrument used to transfer the pattern to the painting surface. It leaves no mark, so the pattern can be used many times.

Surface Conditioner for Air-Dry Enamel Paint is an undercoat that primes and conditions nonporous surfaces, such as tile, glass and ceramics, before applying air-dry enamel paint.

Textile Medium is a medium used with acrylic paints for painting fabrics. By blending this medium with acrylic paint, fabric can be painted and laundered. Always follow the manufacturer's instructions.

Thinner Diluant is a dilutant used to thin air-dry enamel paint. Never use water; water will break down the compound of the paint.

Water-Based Varnish is a protectant used to seal acrylic paint.

BASIC PAINTING TECHNIQUES

Now that you have all of your supplies, there are a few basic brush strokes you must learn. The following techniques are a general overview for the brush strokes used in all of the projects.

⋆How to Load Your Brush

The first thing you must learn is how to add paint to your brush. Depending on the look you want to achieve, there are several ways to load your brush.

Loading Your Flat or Angle Brush

A flat or angle brush is most commonly used for basecoating. The size of the brush is determined by the amount of area you need to cover. In order to get the best coverage and the most out of your brushes, load the paint properly.

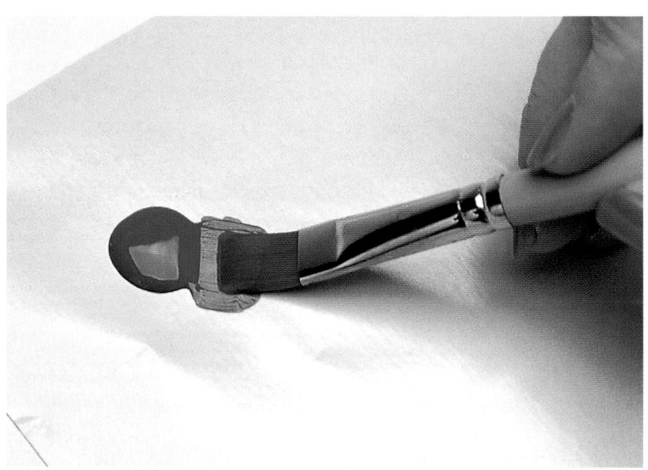

▲ Using a damp brush, pull paint from the edge of your paint puddle. Then, flip the brush over and repeat on the other side. Don't let the paint get up to the ferrule, as this will ruin your brush.

Making a Wash

A wash of color is often used to tint an area of a design. This diluted value of color is transparent and gives a glossy look.

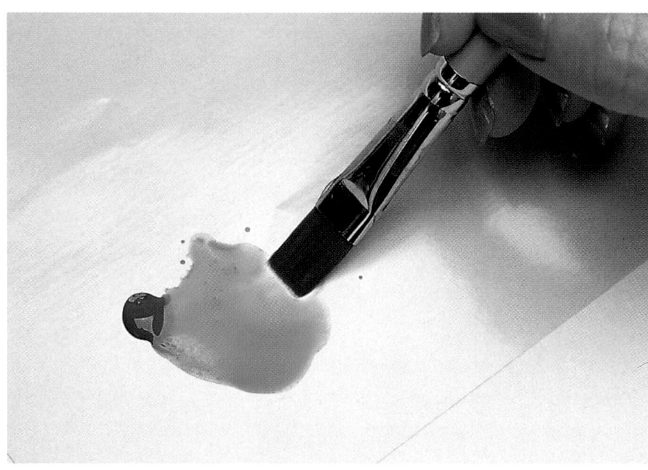

▲ Dip your flat brush in water, and pull a little paint from the edge of your paint puddle. Work the water with the tiny bit of paint to make a puddle of colored water. Rinse and blot the brush, and then load your brush with the wash to paint.

Loading Your Liner

Use a liner when painting thin lines, small details or letters. The size of the liner determines the size of the line.

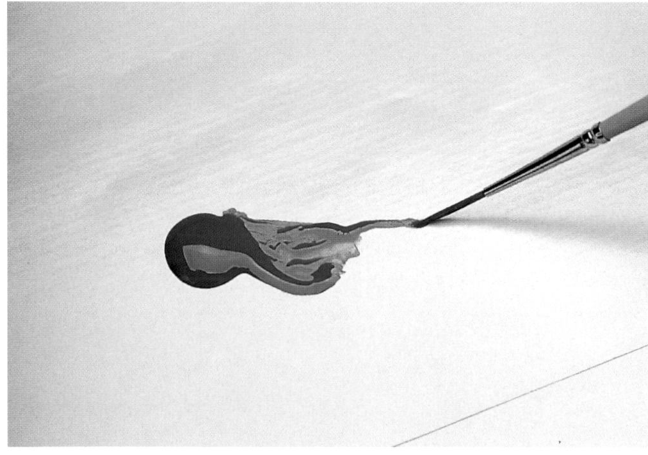

▶ Dip your liner into water, and do not blot. Pull a little bit of paint from the edge of your paint puddle. Mix the water with the paint until you achieve an ink-like consistency.

How to Corner-Load Your Brush

Floating color is a fundamental technique for craft painters, which requires a side- or corner-load application of paint. When you side-load your brush, you apply paint to one corner of the brush, and the color softens and diffuses out to the other side of the brush.

Corner-Load Float

This technique creates depth and dimension in your design. When you corner load your brush and float a darker color, you create a shadow. When you use a lighter color, you create a highlight.

1 Use a flat or angle brush for floating, but make sure your brush still has a chisel edge. Touch the corner of the brush into your paint puddle.

2 With a firm stroke, pull the brush toward you. Do this several times in the same spot.

3 Turn the brush over. With a firm stroke, push the brush away from you. Repeat this several times in the same spot. It's important to do this in the same spot so that the paint remains in the brush and you don't end up painting your palette.

Back-to-Back Float

This technique is basically two side-load floats back-to-back. This creates a highlight in the center of the design and gives the project dimension.

1 Load brush as you did for a side-load float. Apply the edge of the brush along the center of area to be highlighted.

2 Flip your brush over. Apply color on the other side of the highlighted center, backing up to the float you already made. Let dry. Repeat as necessary to build a stronger highlight.

Other Brushstrokes

There are many other specialty brush strokes you can learn. The following will add variety to your projects.

C-Stroke

This brush stroke refers to the direction your side-loaded brush takes. You actually form a C. This stroke is useful when painting curly ringlets, for instance.

1 With a side-load application of color, start on the chisel edge of the brush.

2 Apply pressure to draw the letter C.

3 Release pressure to return to the chisel edge and complete the C.

One Stroke (Leaf Stroke)

This brush stroke is a simple way to paint a basic leaf without shading or highlighting.

1 Load your filbert brush with paint. Apply pressure while the brush is flat.

2 Release pressure as you turn to the chisel edge.

Comma Stroke

This decorative stroke can be done with a liner or a flat brush. Comma strokes are perfect for painting facial feature details and highlights.

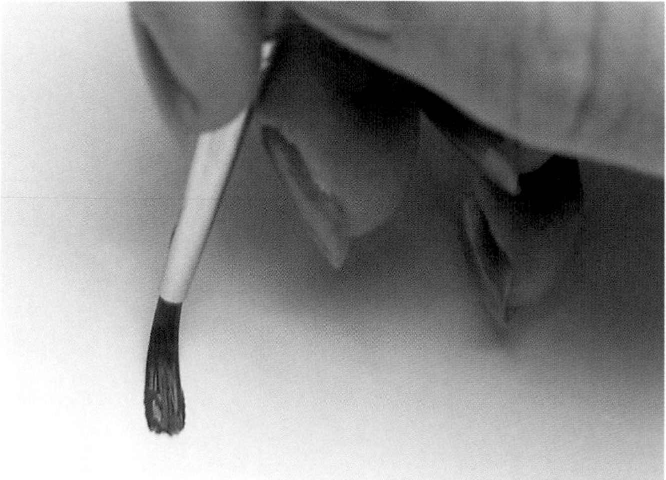

1 Load your liner or round brush generously with paint. Apply pressure at head of stroke.

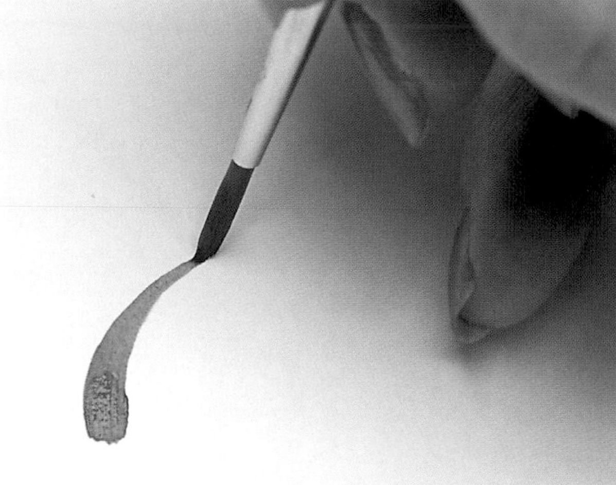

2 Release pressure to paint the tail of the stroke.

Painting Techniques

These painting techniques will give your projects originality and a finishing touch. Although the techniques add complexity and dimension to your painting, you will notice that they are simple, even for the beginner.

Spattering Technique

This technique is done to soften a background or to give the effect of snow.

1 Load your fan brush. Hold the brush firmly in your left hand. Touch the brush to a paper towel before spattering so you do not get globs of paint when you splatter.

2 With your palette knife in your right hand, tap on the ferrule of the fan brush. The paint will spatter over your surface. You may want to try spattering on a scrap of paper before applying paint to your project. This will show you how hard to tap and how much paint you will need. ⋆ **Note:** *If you are left-handed, hold the brush in your right hand and the palette knife in your left.*

Scrubbing Technique

This technique, also known as drybrushing, is used to softly highlight an area or add blush color to a cheek.

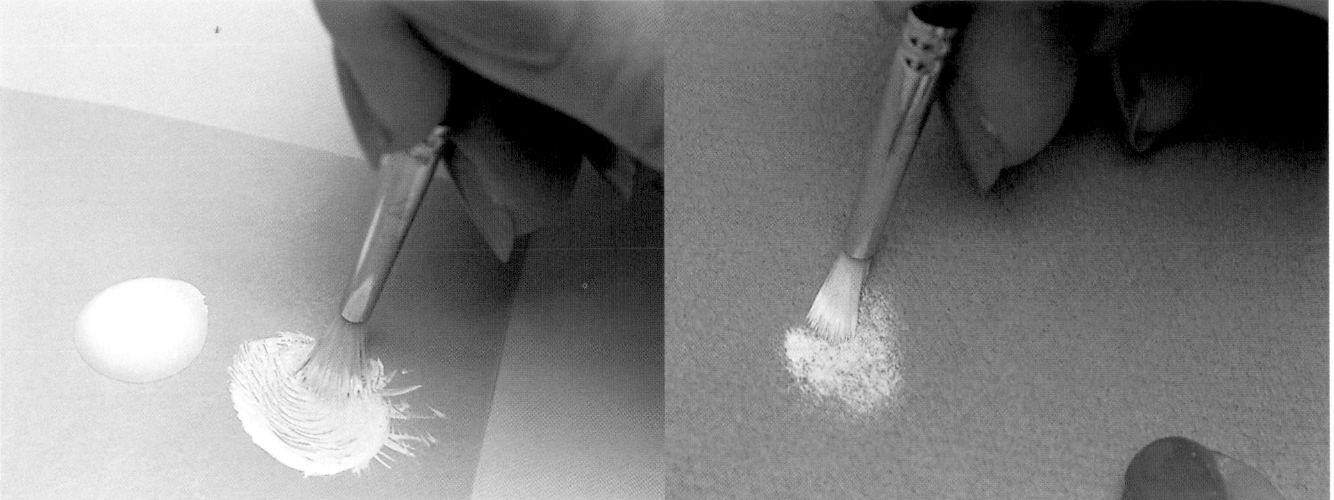

1 Using a scrubber brush, apply paint to the brush on your palette.

2 Next, scrub your brush on a dry paper towel until you have most of the paint out. With a light touch, scrub on your highlight in a circular motion. As you continue, you may increase your pressure.

Stippling Technique

This technique adds color and texture, and is excellent for painting snow on trees, for instance.

◀ There are several brushes you can use to stipple: a mop brush, a Bobbi's Blender or a deerfoot, among others. If you are using one of these, load paint onto a dry brush. If you are using a sable brush, load paint on a damp brush. Dip your brush into the paint puddle and then pounce on your palette to remove the excess paint. Stipple in an up and down motion with a light touch.

Checkerboard Technique

The checkerboard makes a great decorative border. This technique shows you how to make a perfect checkerboard without the use of a stencil or pattern.

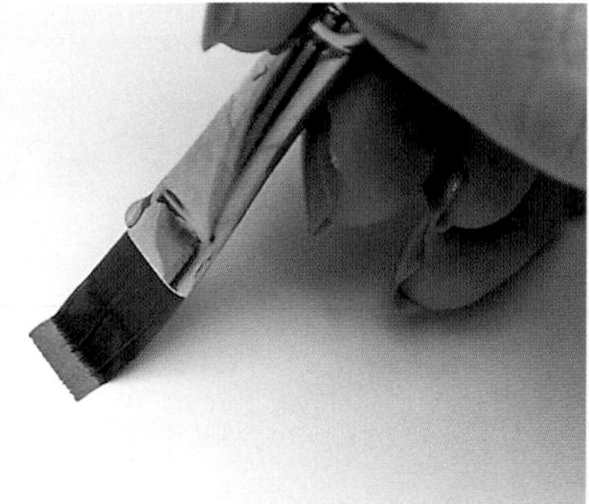

1 The size of the check depends on the size of your brush. Choose the flat brush of your choice and load it with paint. Holding your brush horizontally, make a small stroke. This is the vertical length of your check.

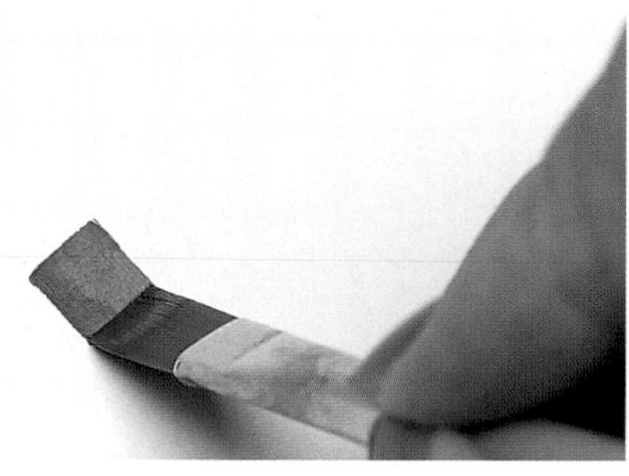

2 Next, holding your brush vertically, lay the brush at the top of the previous stroke. Pull it down as far as the first stroke. This is the horizontal length of your check. You should have a complete square.

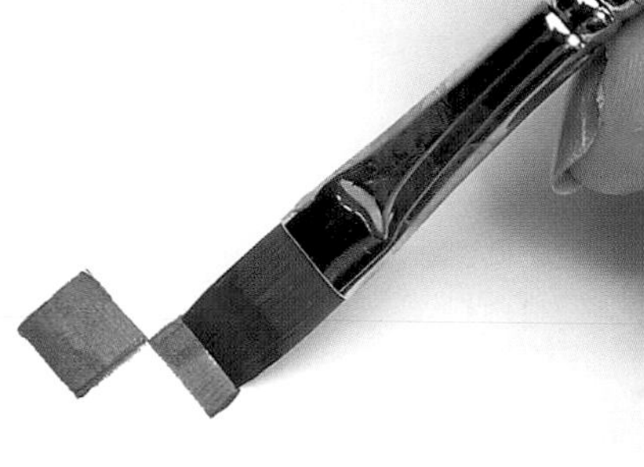

3 Starting at the bottom right corner, repeat your first stroke.

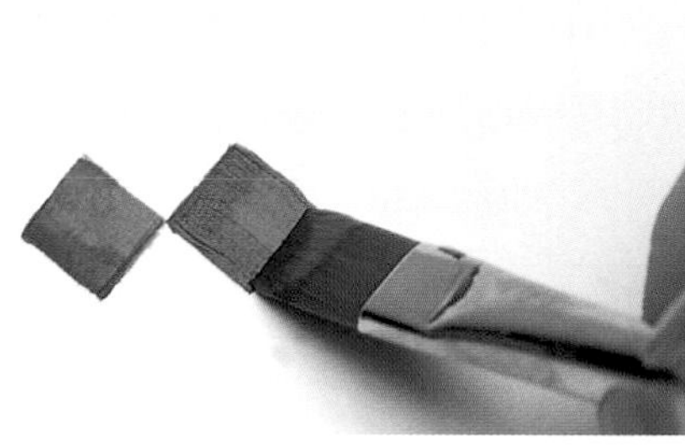

4 Repeat the second stroke so that there are two squares.

5 For the next check, start at the upper right corner and make another square.

6 Repeat, alternating the two rows, as often as you need to complete the checkerboard.

PREPARING SURFACES

In this book, we chose to paint on a variety of mediums. Before you begin painting, be sure to prepare the surface so the paint adheres.

Candle

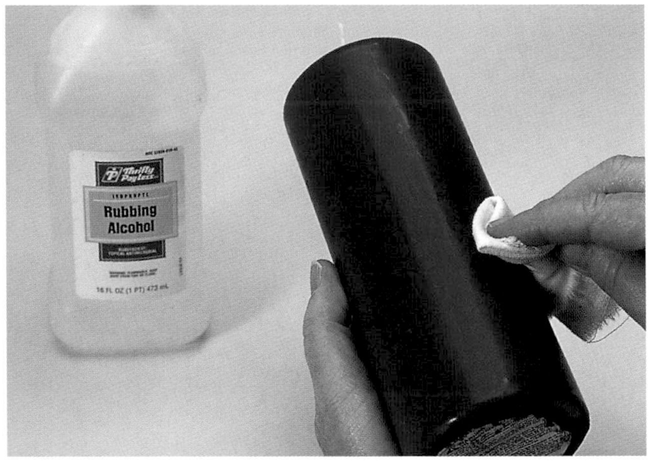

To prepare the candle for painting, first clean the surface with rubbing alcohol. Be careful not to handle the area that will be painted. Mix equal parts of candle and soap painting medium and acrylic paint. Paint the desired area, and let it dry thoroughly.

Fabric

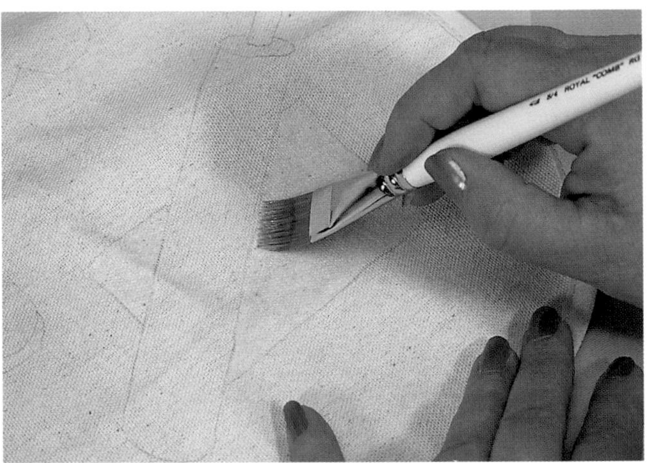

In this book we used only tightly woven fabric, and transferred the pattern using either a stylus and graphite paper, or an iron-on technique. Be sure to prepare the fabric with a layer of textile medium before painting. When the textile medium is still wet, apply the paint. By blending these two products, fabric can be painted and laundered. Paint the desired area, and let it dry thoroughly.

Glass

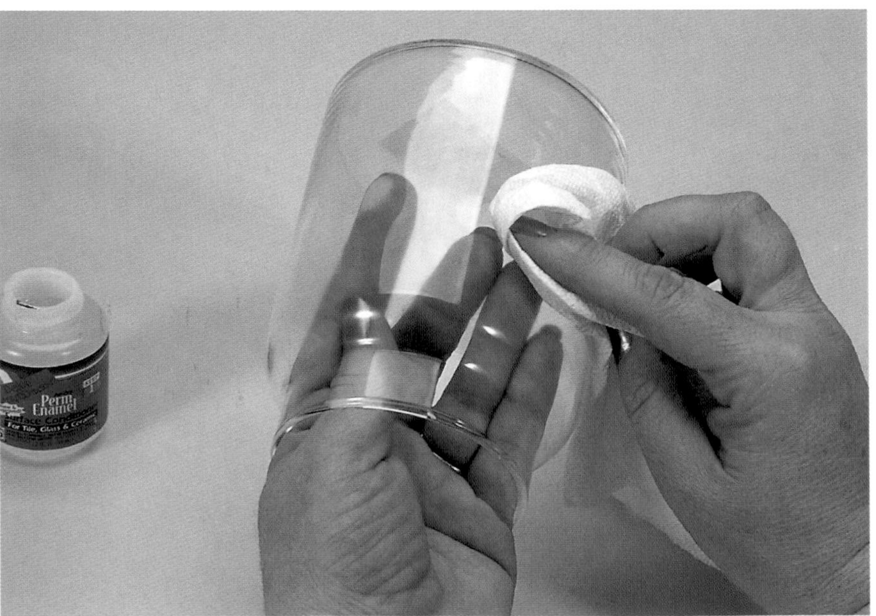

Wash and dry your glass piece. With a paper towel and surface conditioner, wipe the surface. Be careful not to handle the area that will be painted. Let it dry thoroughly before painting.

Wood

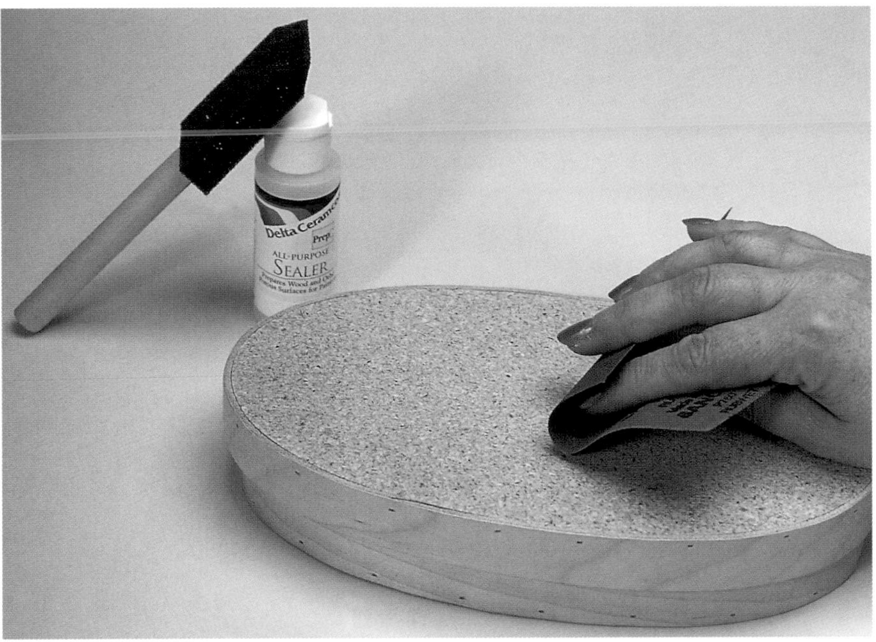

To prepare wood for painting, sand the wood with a medium- to fine- grade sandpaper or a sanding pad. Next, seal the wood with a sealer or a water-based varnish. Finish by lightly sanding the wood.

Metal

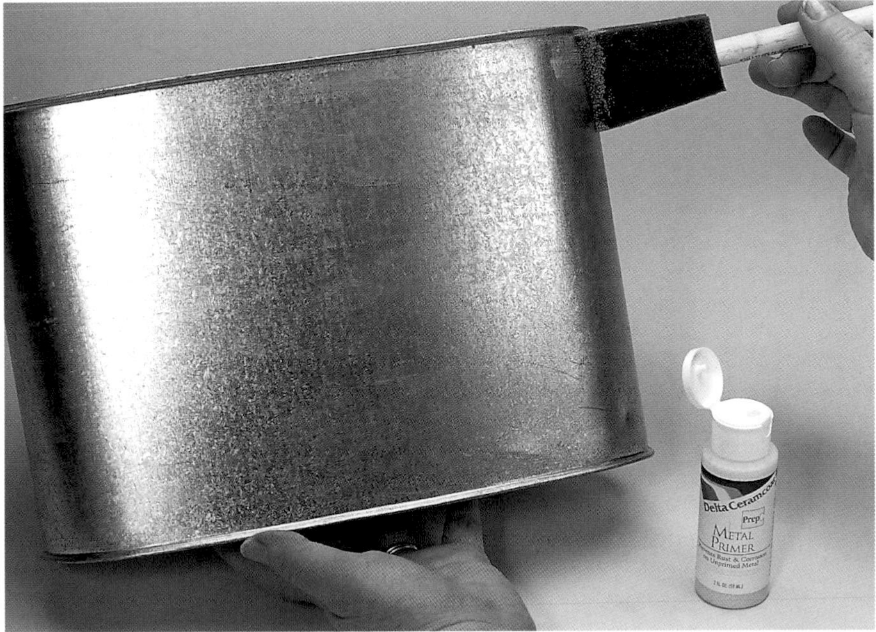

Clean the metal so that it is free from dirt, grease or rust. Basecoat with metal primer. Let it dry for one hour.

8.8fl.oz

Projects

Angels, Christmas trees, gingerbread men... **The projects featured in this book will definitely get you in the Christmas spirit! The step-by-step instructions and templates take all of the difficulty out of craft painting. In no time, you will create these charming projects to decorate your home or give away as Christmas gifts. We are sure that you will find craft painting an enjoyable and therapeutic pastime, and that the projects you make will spread Christmas cheer to your family and friends. So let's get started!**

Note: *In order to use the templates in this book, photocopy the pattern onto tracing paper or acetate, and then transfer the design onto the project surface with graphite transfer paper and your stylus.*

SANTA CANDLE

What could be more fun than a cheerful Santa greeting you during the holiday season? This easy project will be a hit. Surround him with a few shorter, different-colored candles and you will have a delightful centerpiece. Or paint him on cards, ornaments and gift ties for those special friends.

materials:

8" (20cm) Red pillar candle with 2½" (6cm) diameter

Candle and soap painting medium

Rubbing alcohol

Soft cloth

Black and white graphite transfer paper

Stylus

*

BRUSHES

½-inch (12mm) flat

no. 8 flat

no. 2 liner

5/0 liner

small Bobbi's Blender

¼-inch (6mm) comb

¼-inch (6mm) deerfoot

no. 8 filbert

DELTA CERAMCOAT ACRYLIC PAINT

Adobe Red

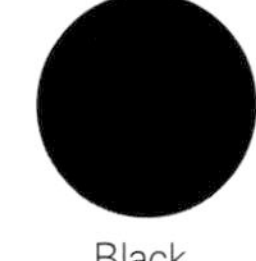
Black

Burnt Sienna

Candy Bar Brown

Dark Foliage Green

Fire Red

Medium Flesh

Perfect Highlight for Red

Quaker Grey

Seminole Green

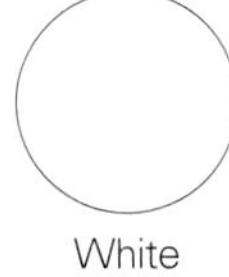
White

Enlarge or reduce this template to fit your project.

1 Prepare the Candle for Painting

Using a soft cloth, wipe down the candle with rubbing alcohol. Let stand approximately one hour, being careful not to touch the area to be painted.

2 Transfer the Pattern

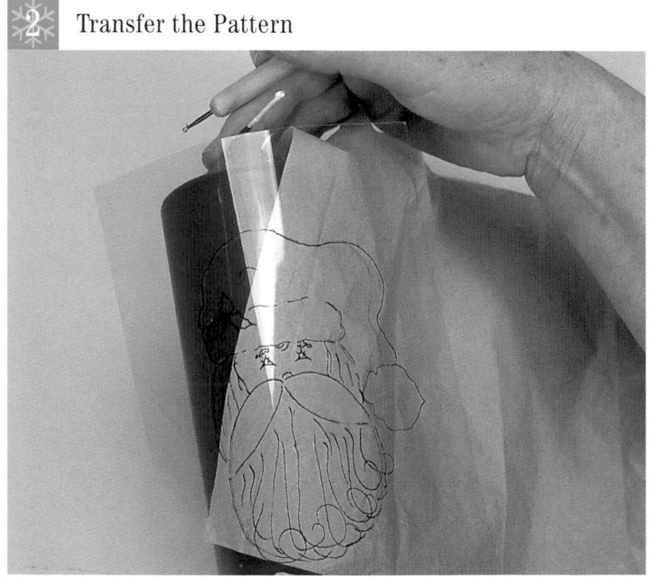

Using your stylus and white graphite paper, transfer the pattern onto the candle.

3 Basecoat the Face and Beard

Mix equal parts of the candle and soap painting medium and Medium Flesh paint, and basecoat the face using your no. 8 filbert. Mix the Quaker Grey paint with the candle and soap painting medium, and basecoat the beard and hair with your ½-inch (12mm) flat.

4 Basecoat the Fur

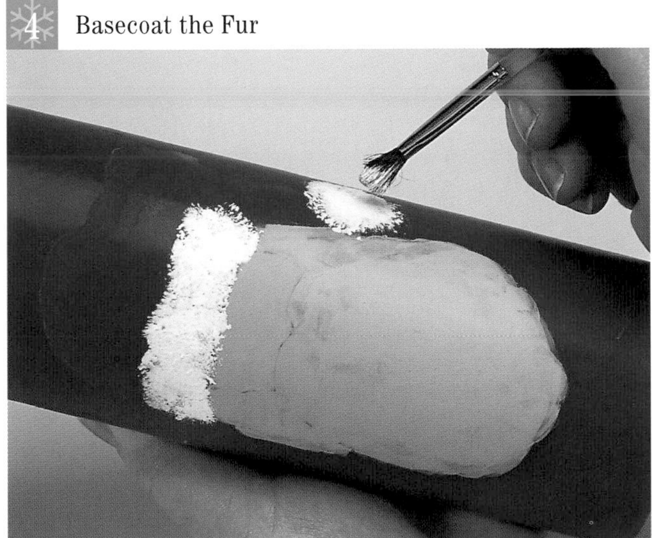

Mix the candle and soap painting medium with White, and using the small Bobbi's Blender, stipple in the fur. This will take two coats.

5 Add Santa's Hat

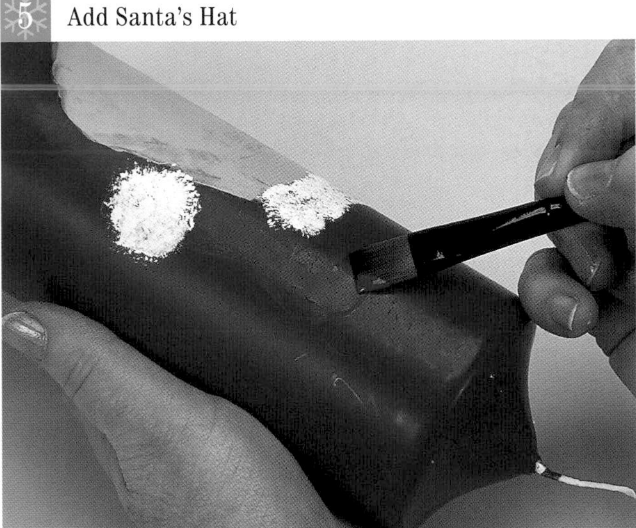

Mix the candle and soap painting medium with Perfect Highlight for Red. Corner-load the brush, and float around the edge of the hat with your ½-inch (12mm) flat. The red color of the candle will be the base color for the hat.

6 Transfer the Facial Features

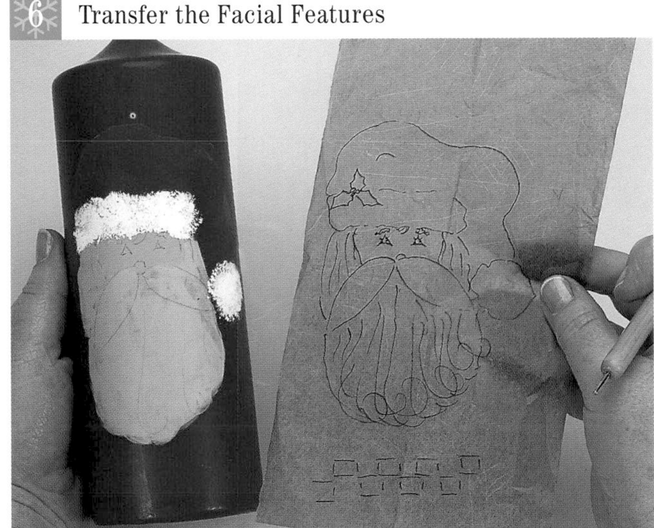

Using black graphite transfer paper and stylus, apply the facial features to the face.

7 Shade the Hat

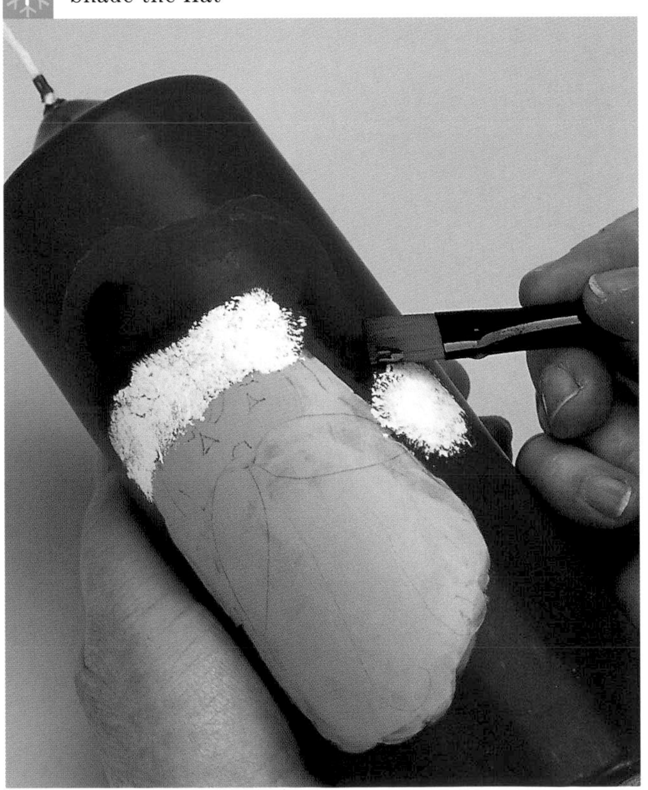

Mix the candle and soap painting medium with Candy Bar Brown paint. Corner-load your ½" (12mm) flat, and float a shade just above the fur and just above the pom. Float in a fold near the top of the hat and next to the face on the right side.

8 Add the Facial Features

With your 5/0 liner and Black paint, add the eyes and lashes. Tap in a White highlight at two and seven o'clock in each eye. Add the eyebrows using White paint. With the same brush, add the nose with Burnt Sienna and the mouth with Candy Bar Brown.

HINT

It is necessary to add the candle and soap painting medium only when you are painting directly onto the candle.

9 Scrub on the Cheek Color

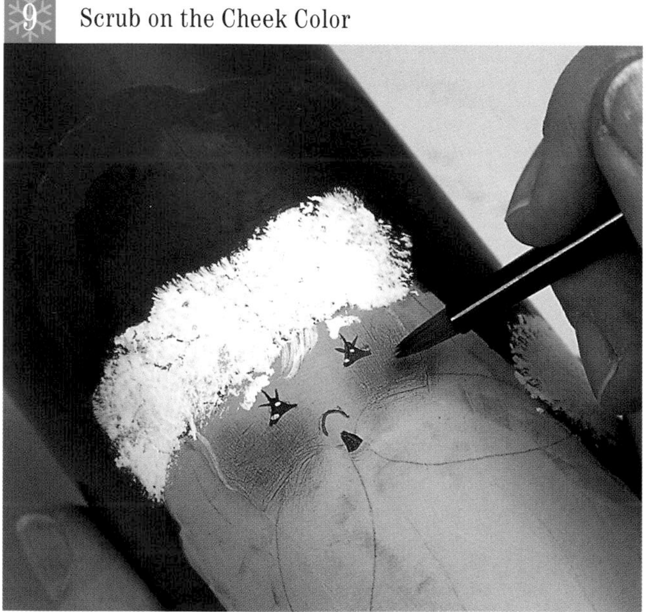

Using your deerfoot brush and Adobe Red, drybrush the cheeks. Use a light touch here so that you do not scratch the base surface.

10 Detail the Beard

Using White and your ¼-inch (6 mm) comb brush, add details to the beard. Start in the middle and work your way to each side. Add a few curls at the end of the beard.

11 Detail the Mustache

With your no. 2 liner, outline the mustache. Add lines starting in the middle. Follow the contour of the mustache.

12 Add the Holly

Using your no. 2 liner, basecoat the holly leaves on the hat with equal parts of Seminole Green and Dark Foliage Green. Add berries with Fire Red with the end of your stylus.

13 Add Checkerboard

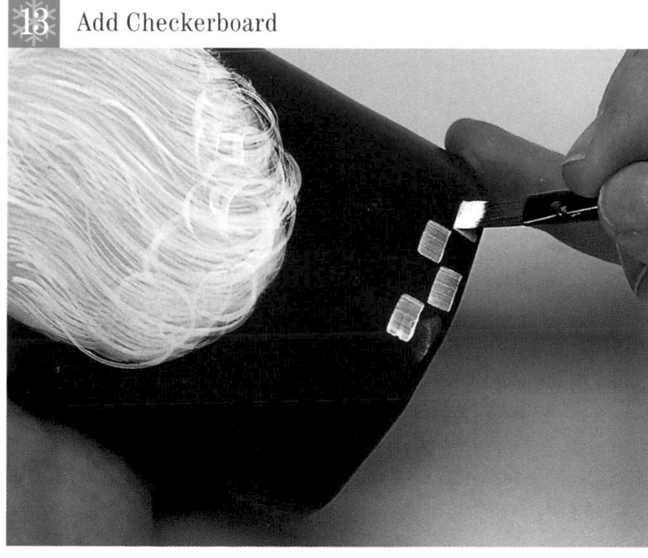

Mix White with the candle and soap painting medium, and using your no. 8 flat, add the checks at the top and bottom of the candle.

When you finish painting the Santa Candle, apply a coat of soap and candle painting medium to protect the finish and give it a glossy look.

PEPPERMINT STICK CANDY JAR

Who doesn't love candy canes at Christmastime? This is the perfect jar for candy canes or any holiday candy. The pattern will work on any smooth-sided jar. And when you have trouble keeping the jar filled with candy, it will still look good.

materials:

Glass jar with lid

Surface conditioner

Thinner diluant

Clear Gloss Glaze

Craft glue

Gold rickrack

Candy for top

Black graphite transfer paper

Stylus

★

BRUSHES

⅜-inch (10mm) angle

no. 12 flat

no. 1 liner

¾-inch (19mm) glaze

DELTA CERAMDECOR AIR-DRY PERMENAMEL

Midnight

Red Red

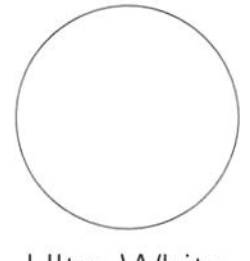

Ultra White

Enlarge or reduce this template to fit your project.

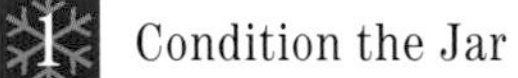

Condition the Jar

Using a paper towel and the surface conditioner, wipe the entire jar. Let it dry, and be careful not to put your fingers on the jar.

Transfer Pattern

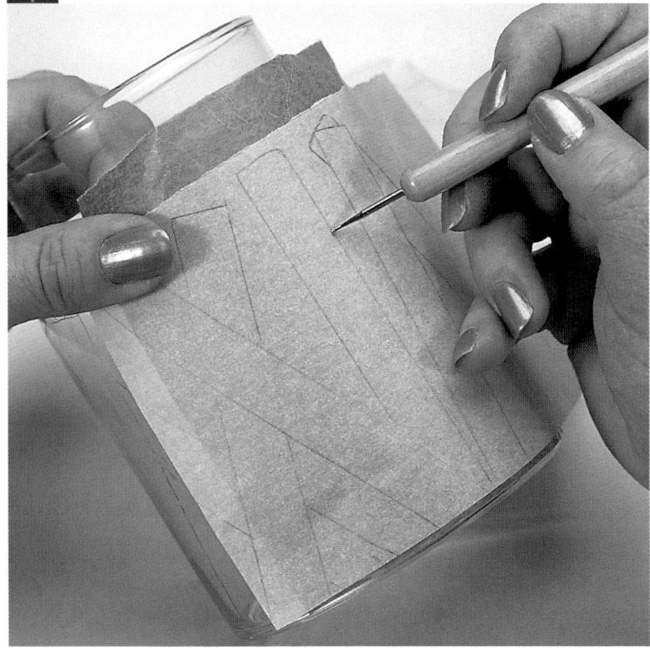

Using a stylus and black graphite transfer paper, trace the pattern onto the jar.

3 Basecoat the Candy Sticks

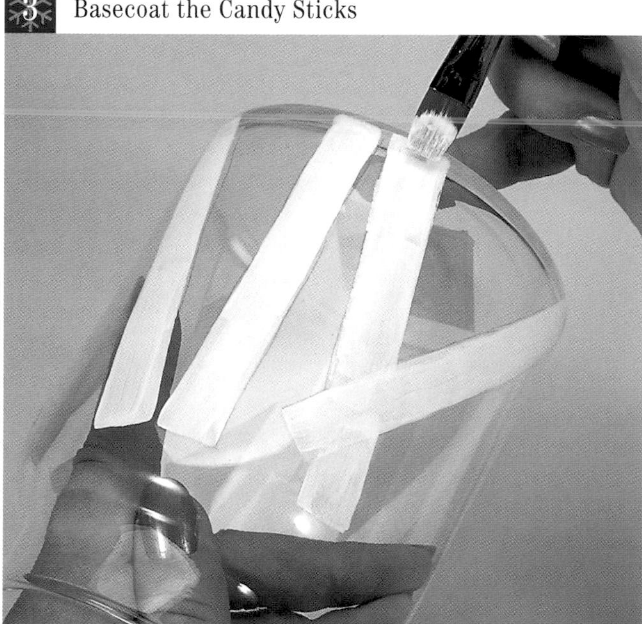

Using Ultra White and your no. 12 flat, basecoat each stick. This may require two coats.

HINT

If you use a hair dryer to speed up your drying time, be sure the glass is cool before painting the next coat, or the paint will dry too fast.

4 Add Red Stripes

Using the no. 12 flat, paint red stripes using Red Red.

5 Detail With Thin Stripes

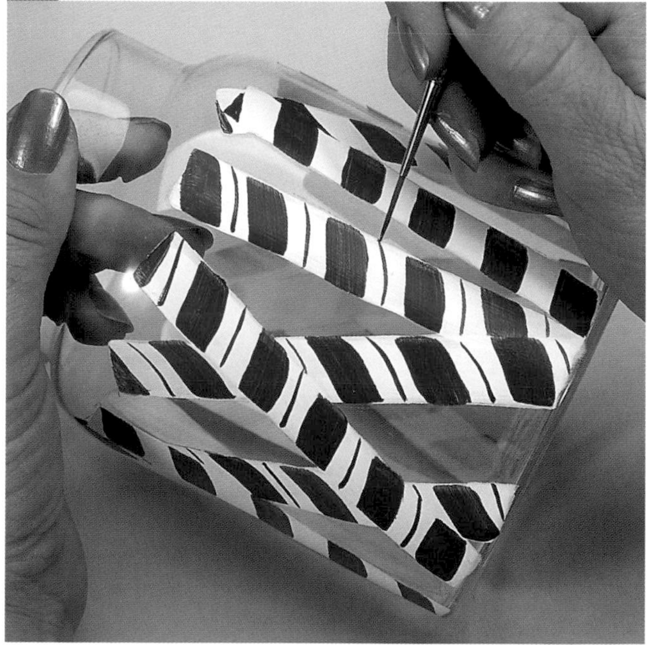

Add the narrow stripes between the larger stripes, using a no. 1 liner and Red Red.

6 Shade the Candy Stick

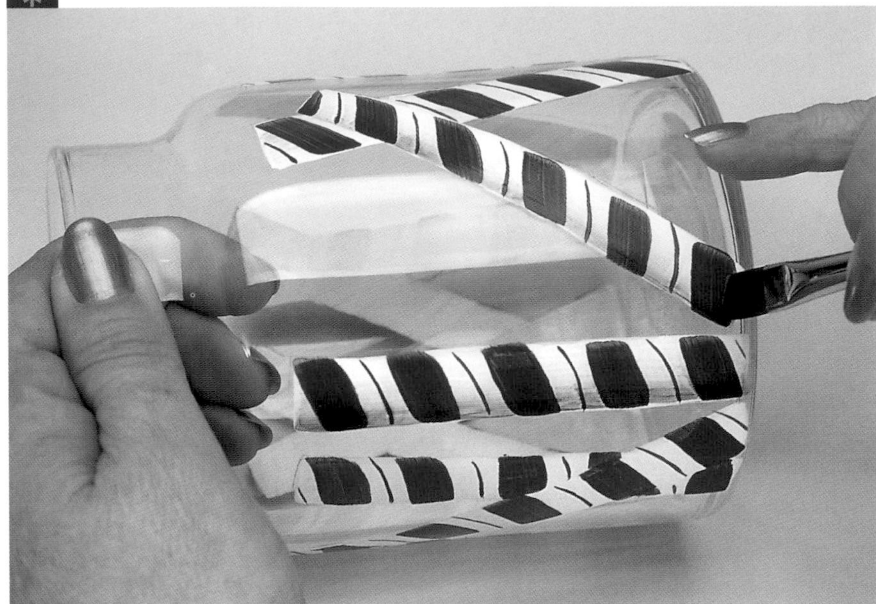

Place a drop of thinner on your palette and a drop of Midnight. Load thinner in your ⅜-inch (10mm) angle, and corner-load the Midnight. Float down the left side to shade each candy stick.

7 Separate the Overlapping Canes

When there are two sticks touching or crossing over each other, shade the cane that is in the back.

8 Highlight the Candy

With your no. 1 liner brush and Ultra White, place a highlight line down the center. Allow the line to skip every so often, and don't let your line touch the outer edges.

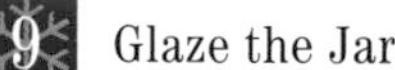

9 Glaze the Jar

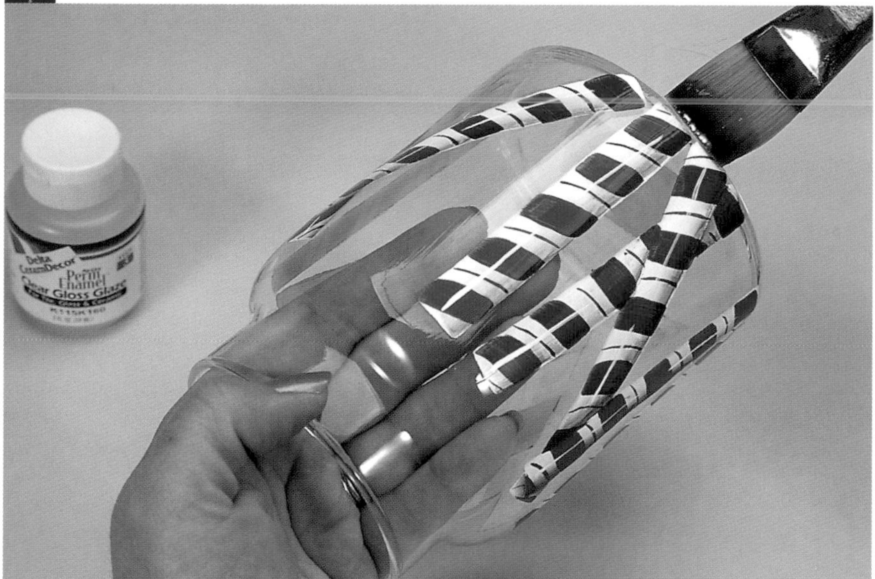

With a ¾-inch (19mm) glaze brush and the clear gloss glaze, paint over the entire area. Don't stroke over it.

When the Peppermint Candy Jar is dry, glue on gold rick-rack and fill lid with candy. When necessary, handwash the jar. Do not put it in the dishwasher.

SANTA MOON SAUCER

For this adorable project, I used an ordinary clay saucer. You could use any size saucer you like and adjust the pattern accordingly. This would make a great teacher or neighbor gift filled with goodies. On Christmas Eve, fill this saucer with cookies for Santa.

materials

8" (20cm) Terra-cotta saucer
Water-based varnish
Black and white graphite transfer paper
Stylus

BRUSHES

½-inch (12mm) angle
⅜-inch (10mm) angle
¾-inch (19mm) flat
no. 12 flat
no. 6 flat
no. 3 round
no. 1 liner
10/0 liner
no. 2 scrubber

DELTA CERAMCOAT ACRYLIC PAINT

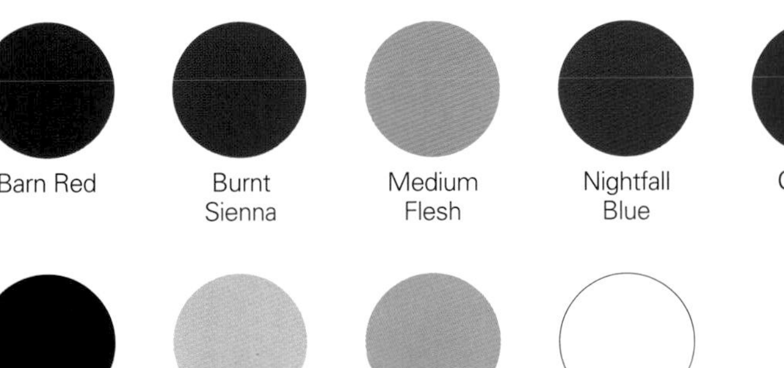

Barn Red
Burnt Sienna
Medium Flesh
Nightfall Blue
Opaque Red

Paynes Grey

Raw Linen

Straw

White

Enlarge or reduce this template to fit your project.

1 Paint the Background

With a ¾-inch (19mm) flat brush, basecoat the saucer with Nightfall Blue. Be sure to cover all surface areas. Transfer pattern onto saucer with white graphite transfer paper and your stylus.

2 Basecoat the Santa

Using your no. 12 flat, basecoat the face with two to three coats of Medium Flesh, the hat with three coats of Opaque Red, the hatband with one to two coats of Barn Red and the beard with three coats of Raw Linen. Using your no. 6 flat brush, basecoat the star with one to two coats of Straw and the moon with one to two coats of equal parts Straw and Raw Linen. When dry, transfer the facial features onto the saucer with black graphite transfer paper and a stylus.

3 Paint the Plaid

Using your no. 1 liner and White, paint diagonal lines going in the same direction. Then go back and paint all the lines going in the opposite direction. When you are finished, you should have diamond shapes. Next, use Straw that is thinned with a little water, and paint a stripe on both sides of the White stripe. Finally, with your no. 1 liner, paint vertical stripes on the hatband with equal parts of Paynes Grey and Barn Red.

4 Shade the Face

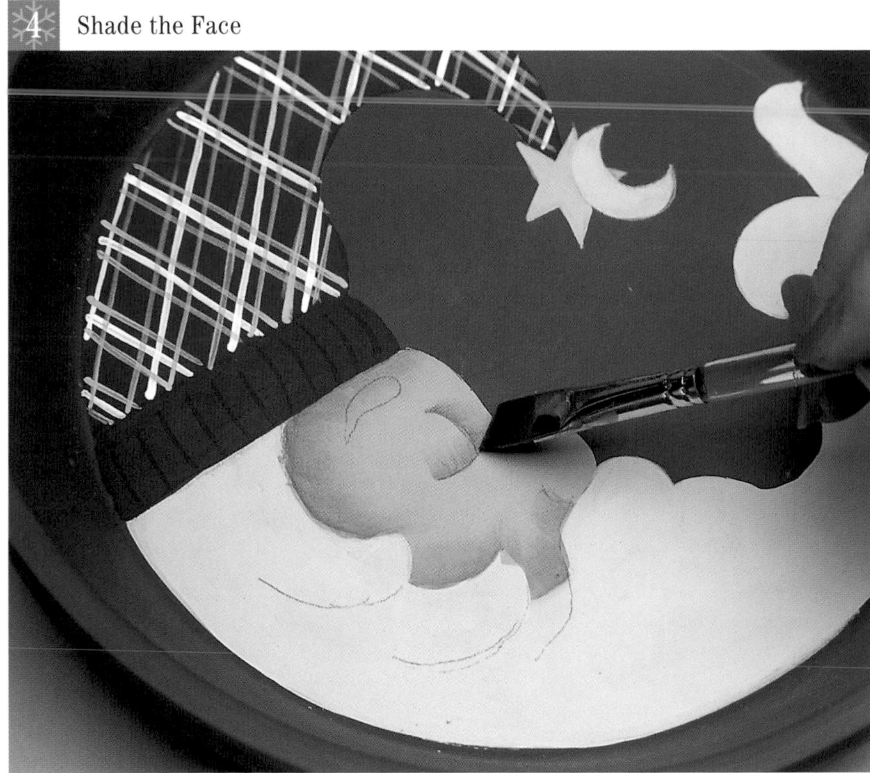

With Burnt Sienna and your ½-inch (12mm) angle, float around the face, along the eyelid and on the back of the nose.

5 Shade the Hat

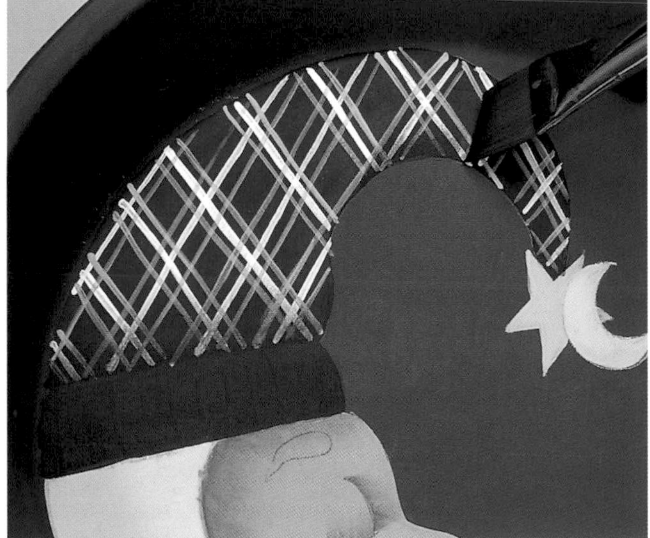

With Paynes Grey and your ½-inch (12mm) angle, float along the top and bottom of the hatband and in the crook of the hat, down to the star and moon.

6 Shade the Eyebrow, the Beard, the Hair and the Star

Using your no. 3 round and Raw Linen, add the eyebrow. Shade the beard and hair with Paynes Grey, using your ½-inch (12mm) angle. Float under the hatband, the underside of each curl, under the nose, under the mustache and the outside edge of the hat, hatband and beard. Then, with your ⅜-inch (10mm) angle, shade the star with Burnt Sienna, separating it from the moon.

7 Detail the Face

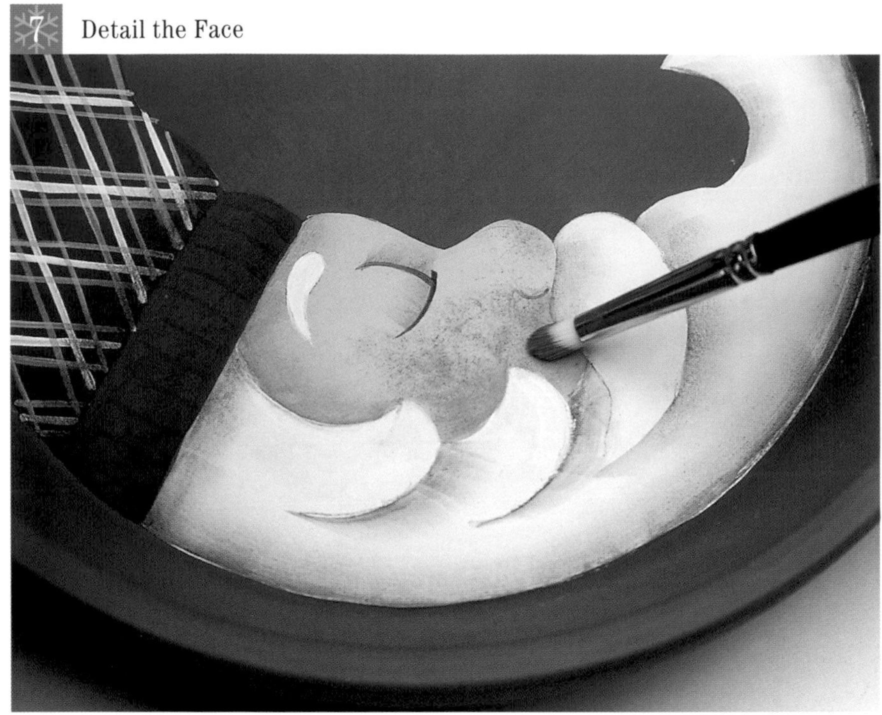

Using your scrubber brush, mix equal parts of Medium Flesh and Opaque Red and scrub on the cheeks. Start next to the beard and work toward the eye. Also scrub a little color on the end of the nose. Paint an eyelid and nostril with your 10/0 liner and thinned Burnt Sienna. Use Paynes Grey for the lash line.

8 Highlight the Beard and Moon

Using the ½-inch (12mm) angle and White, float along the tops of each curl of Santa's hair and beard. With your ⅜-inch (10mm) angle brush, float along the left side of the moon.

9 Add Eyebrow and Mustache Highlights

Using the no. 3 round and White paint, place a comma stroke along the top of the eyebrow. Then add five consecutive comma strokes to form the mustache. Start these at the outside edge and curve toward the nose.

10 Add Background Stars

Dip the handle of a small brush into White paint, and dot it on your background. Dot three to four times and then reload. This will give you the effect of different-sized stars. To make a star twinkle, use your 10/0 liner and draw a vertical line, a horizontal line and then an X through the dot.

Finish the Santa Moon Saucer by sealing with two to three coats of a water-based varnish.

SUGAR
350°
EGGS
3/4 C. SUGAR
3c. Flour
sugars, shortening,

LITTLE HELPER'S APRON

Remember making Christmas cookies as a kid? Now that you are the adult, isn't there a little helper in your family who wants to help out in the kitchen? This is a great gift for that special little person in your life. It's the perfect thing to make a child feel important during this festive time. You can even enlarge the pattern and make one for yourself as well.

materials

Child's apron

Textile medium

Micron .03 permanent pen

Clear ruler

Piece of cardboard (the size of design area) covered in wax paper

Black graphite transfer paper

Stylus

BRUSHES

no. 12 flat

no. 1 liner

¾-inch (19mm) comb

½-inch (12mm) comb

DELTA CERAMCOAT ACRYLIC PAINT

Autumn Brown

Barn Red

Burnt Umber

Raw Sienna

Spice Brown

Tompte Red

White

Enlarge or reduce this template to fit your project.

1 Transfer Pattern

Trace the pattern onto the apron, using black graphite and your stylus.

2 Prepare the Fabric With Textile Medium

Place the cardboard with wax paper under the apron. With your ¾-inch (19mm) comb brush, paint the recipe card with textile medium.

3 Paint the Recipe Card

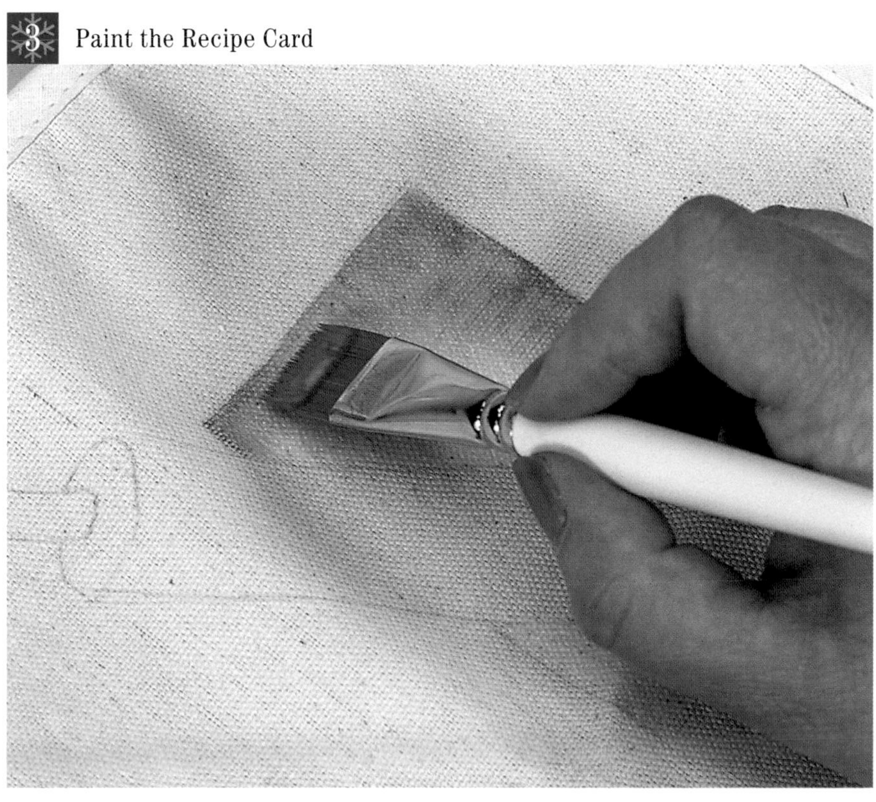

With your ¾-inch (19mm) comb brush and Raw Sienna, paint along the edge of the recipe card and pull the brush toward the center. Work around all four sides. The color should not meet in the middle. Allow this to dry, being careful to keep your hands off of the area.

HINT

Painting the textile medium on the fabric first and then adding the paint is called wet-on-wet. It creates a softer line and makes the painting look more like you used fabric dyes. Whenever you paint directly on the fabric, you should prep the fabric with textile medium.

4 Paint the Gingerbread Cookie

Brush textile medium onto the gingerbread cookie, and then paint with Autumn Brown and your ½-inch (12mm) comb brush. Start on the outside edges and pull toward the center. The color will meet in the center but will be lighter than the outside edges.

5 Shade the Cookie

While the cookie is still wet, side-load your ½-inch (12mm) comb brush with Burnt Umber. Float along the outer edges of the arms, legs and head.

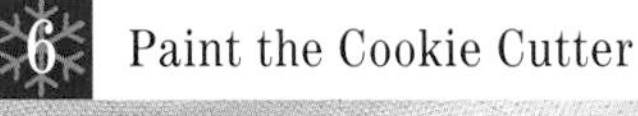

6 Paint the Cookie Cutter

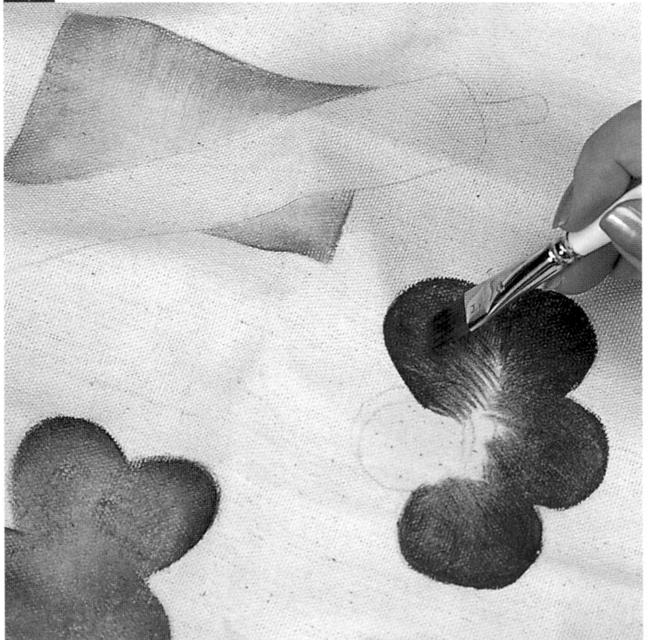

Paint the cookie cutter first with textile medium and your ½-inch (12mm) comb brush. While this is still wet, load your brush with Tompte Red and work from the outer edges toward the center.

7 Shade the Cookie Cutter

With the corner of the same brush, paint the outside edges of the cookie cutter with Barn Red.

8 Shade the Handle

Corner-load your ½-inch (12mm) comb brush, and float on either side of the handle with Barn Red.

9 Basecoat the Rolling Pin

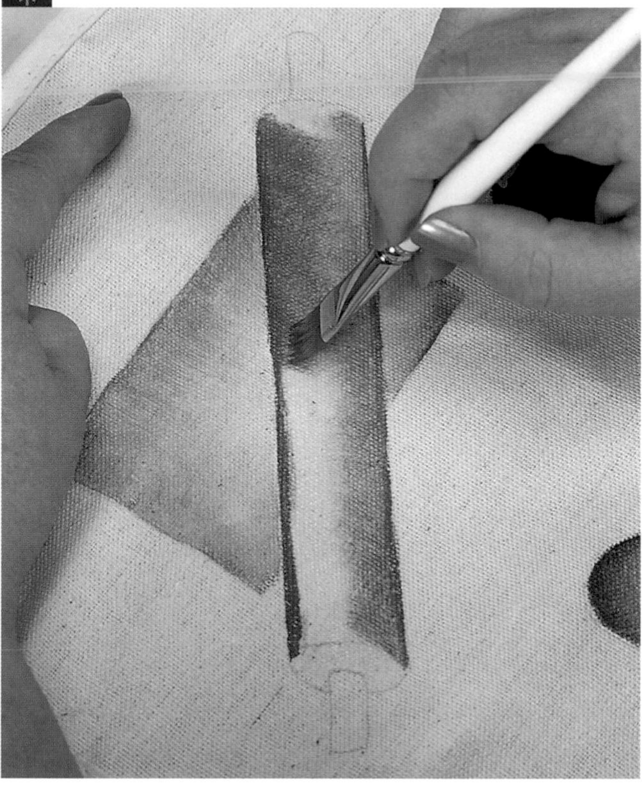

Paint the rolling pin with Spice Brown. Place your ½-inch (12mm) comb brush on the outside edge and stroke toward the center, working across one long side. Turn the apron around and paint the other long side, using the same technique. This helps create the cylinder shape.

10 Shade the Rolling Pin

While your rolling pin is still wet, use your ½-inch (12mm) comb brush to float Burnt Umber on the long edges.

11 Shade Edge of Rolling Pin

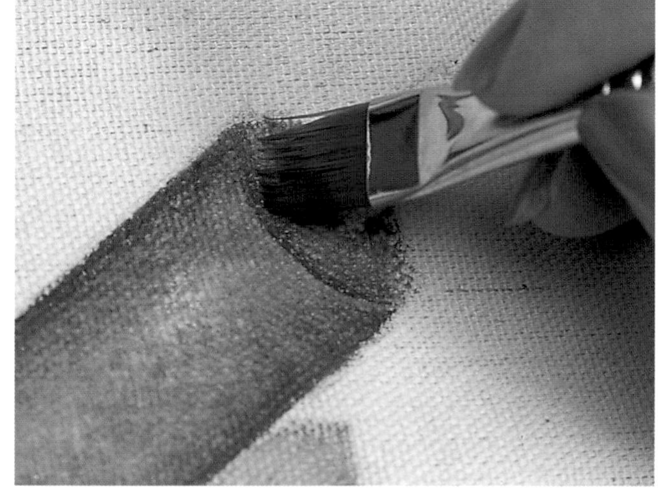

With the same brush and color, float the inside curve of end of the rolling pin. This will give it dimension.

12 Add Handles

Paint the handles of the rolling pin, using your ½-inch (12mm) comb brush and equal parts of Tompte Red and textile medium.

13 Shade Handles

While the handles are still wet, shade with Barn Red and your ½-inch (12mm) comb brush.

14 Add Grain Lines

To create the grain lines, corner-load your ½-inch (12mm) comb brush with Burnt Umber. Use the chisel edge to pull lines down the rolling pin.

15 Shade the Background

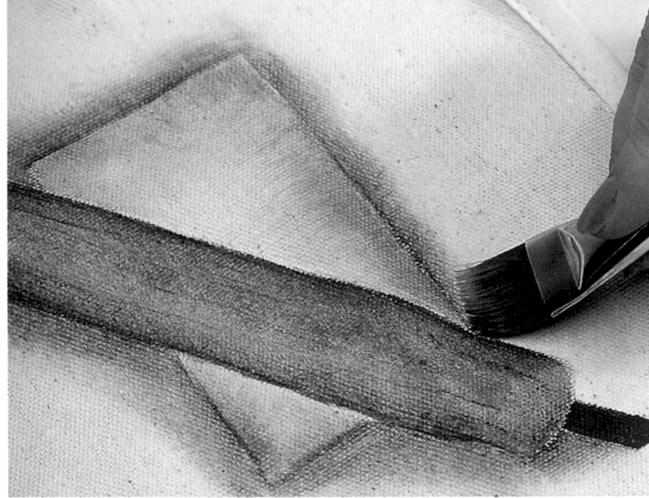

Using your ¾-inch (19mm) comb brush, first load brush with textile medium. Next, corner-load brush with Burnt Umber, and float along the outside of the recipe card, rolling pin, cookie and cookie cutter.

16 Paint Cookie Icing

Thin White paint with a drop of textile medium, and paint a wavy line of icing with your no. 1 liner.

17 Add Eyes and Buttons

Using the handle of a brush and Burnt Umber, add the eyes and buttons on the gingerbread man.

18 Add Nose, Mouth and Bow

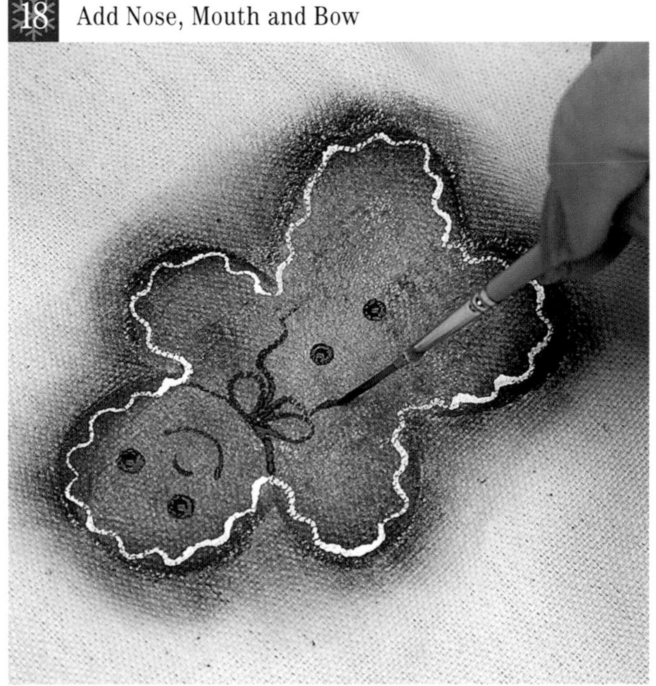

Thin the Burnt Umber with a small amount of textile medium. Using your no. 1 liner, paint on the nose and mouth. Next, thin some Tompte Red with a drop of textile medium, and using your liner, paint a simple bow.

19 Draw Lines on the Recipe Card

When your recipe card is dry, use the permanent pen and the clear ruler to draw your lines.

20 Write the Recipe

With the permanent pen, write your favorite cookie recipe.

21 Add Checkerboard

Use equal parts of Tompte Red and textile medium and load your no. 12 flat brush. Start just above the edge of the binding and continue around the apron. (See complete checkerboard instructions in the techniques section on page 15.)

When the Little Helper's Apron is completely dry, you may want to outline the rolling pin, recipe, cookie cutter and cookie with your permanent pen. Allow the paint to set for a few days, and then wash the apron in cold water.

GINGERBREAD MAN POTHOLDER

This Gingerbread Man Potholder is the perfect complement to the Little Helper's Apron. Iron the gingerbread man's face onto a 7½"(19cm) square potholder using a transfer pen. Prepare the fabric with textile medium before painting. Using your ½-inch (12mm) comb brush, basecoat the face in Autumn Brown and the bowtie and nose in Tompte Red. Corner-load your ½-inch (12mm) comb brush, and shade the bowtie with Black paint. Pounce in the cheeks with your no. 8 sable brush and equal parts of textile medium and Tompte Red. Next, add the eyes with equal parts of textile medium and Black, using your no. 8 filbert. With your no. 1 liner, paint the mouth, and with your no. 2 liner, add comma strokes for the eye-brows. Add a wavy line of icing with your no. 1 liner and equal parts of textile medium and White. Finish by highlighting the eyes, nose and bow tie using small comma strokes.

DELTA CERAMCOAT ACRYLIC PAINT

Autumn Brown

Black

Tompte Red

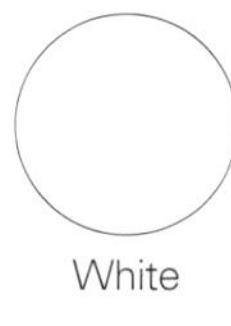
White

Enlarge or reduce this template to fit your project.

GOSSAMER WINGED ANGEL

Whether you have been touched by an angel, have a guardian angel or just love angels, this project is sure to find a special place in your home and heart. This is a great family project to do. Find a quiet place, gather all of the necessary supplies and ask a few friends of all ages to come and paint an angel for the tree. You will surely make some wonderful memories to cherish year round.

materials

9¼" (23cm) Papier-mâché cone with 3" (8cm) diameter

2" (5cm) Head ball

⅜" (1cm) dowel rod

1 yard (91cm) of ¼" (1cm) wide pink ribbon

1 yard (91cm) of 1" (3cm) white lace

Small fabric rose (available at craft stores)

Gold pipe cleaner

Set of gossamer wings (available at craft stores)

Craft glue

Water-based varnish

Black graphite transfer paper

Stylus

BRUSHES

½-inch (12mm) flat

no. 10 flat

no. 2 liner

no. 1 liner

¼-inch (6mm) deerfoot

no. 10 filbert

DELTA CERAMCOAT ACRYLIC PAINT

Adobe Red

Black

Burnt Sienna

Dresden Flesh

Rose Cloud

Rose Mist

Seminole Green

Straw

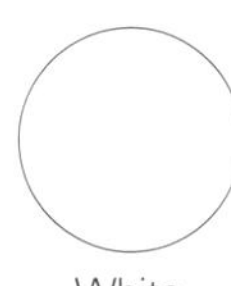
White

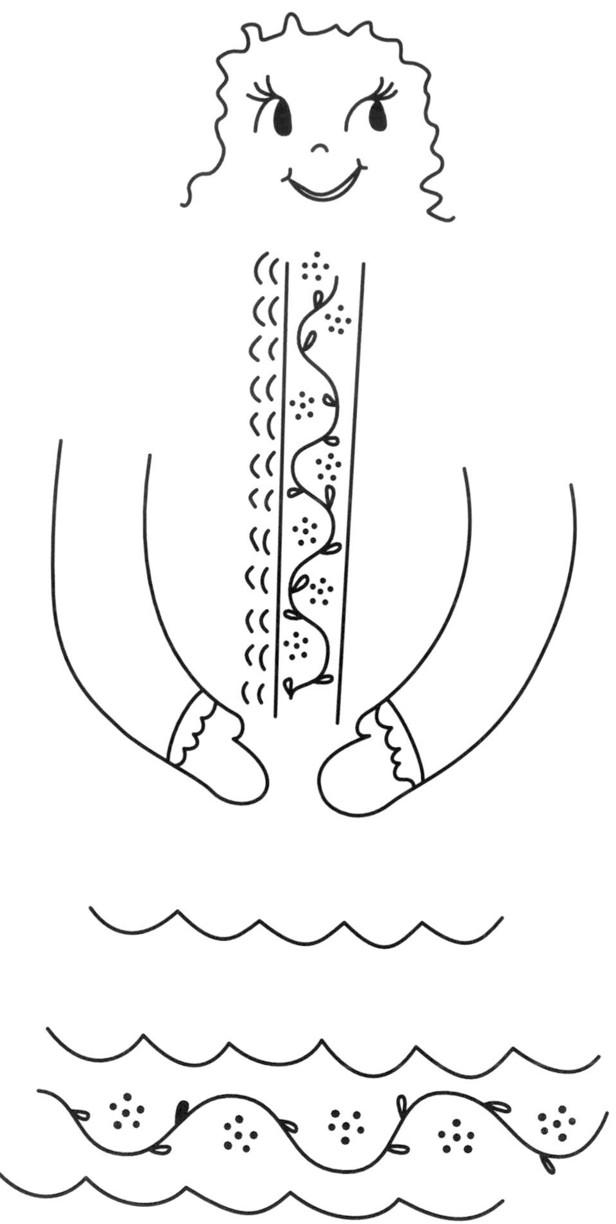

Enlarge or reduce this template to fit your project.

1 Basecoat the Cone and Head

With your ½-inch (12mm) flat brush, basecoat the cone with Rose Cloud and the head with Dresden Flesh. After they dry, transfer the pattern using black graphite transfer paper and a stylus.

2 Shade In Arms

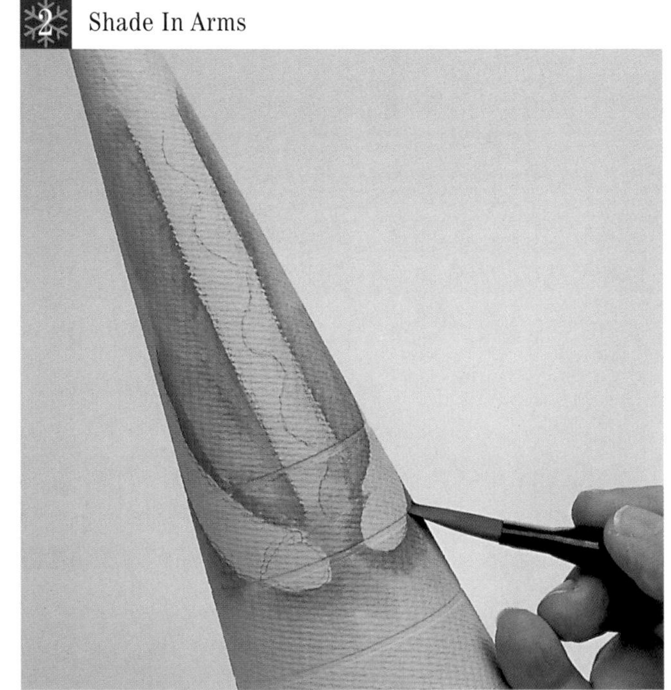

Corner-load your ½-inch (12mm) flat for floated color with Rose Mist, and shade around the arms, hands and front of the dress. Basecoat the hands with Dresden Flesh and your no. 10 filbert.

3 Basecoat the Face

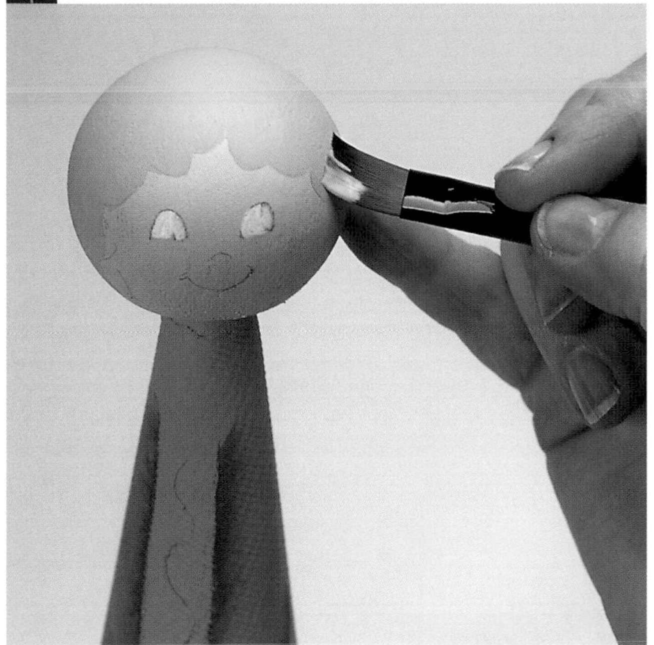

Paint the hair in Straw with your ½-inch (12mm) flat. Using your no. 2 liner and White, basecoat the eyes.

4 Add Angel's Facial Features

With your no. 1 liner, basecoat the eyes and lashes with Black. Continue to use the same brush and add the nose and mouth with Burnt Sienna.

5 Continue to Add Facial Details

Using your no. 1 liner and White, highlight each eye at two o'clock. Widen the lips just a touch with Adobe Red and your no. 1 liner.

6 Paint Cheek Color

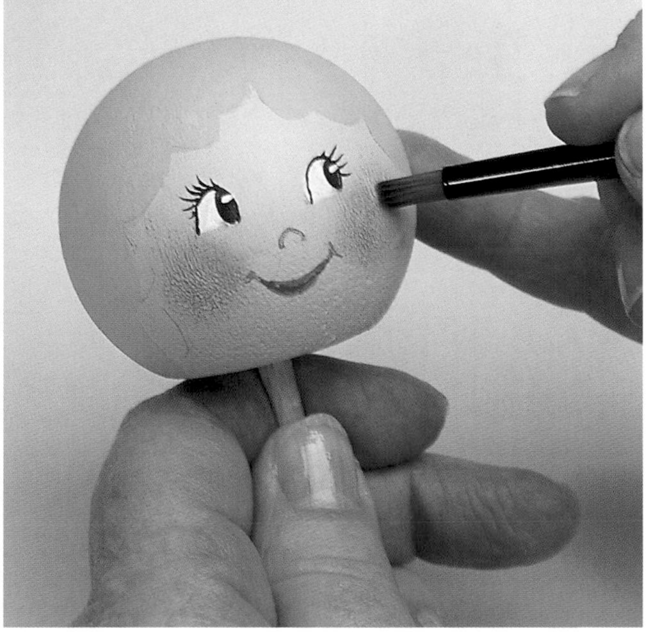

Pick up a very small amount of Adobe Red with your ¼-inch (6mm) deerfoot. Wipe almost all of the color from the brush. Very lightly drybrush the cheeks.

7 Detail the Angel's Hair

This part is really fun. Corner-load the no. 10 flat with Burnt Sienna. Randomly place C-strokes all over the head. Add as many or as few curls as you would like.

8 Add Ruffles to the Dress

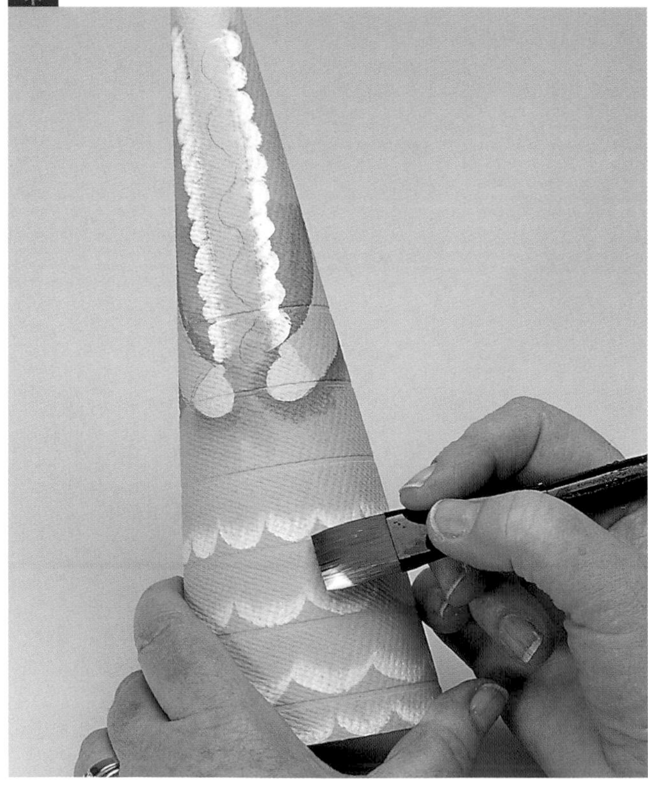

Corner-load your no. 10 flat with White. Float the ruffles down the front and around the bottom of the dress.

9 Paint the Flower Stems on the Dress

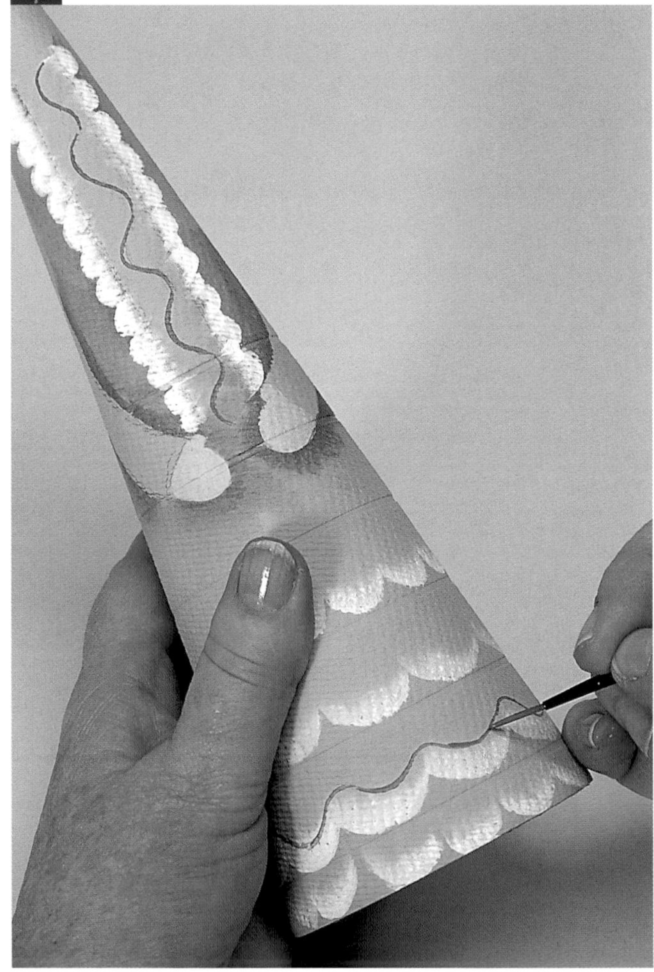

With your no. 2 liner and Seminole Green, add the stems and leaves to the front and the bottom of the dress.

10 Add Flower Blossoms to the Dress

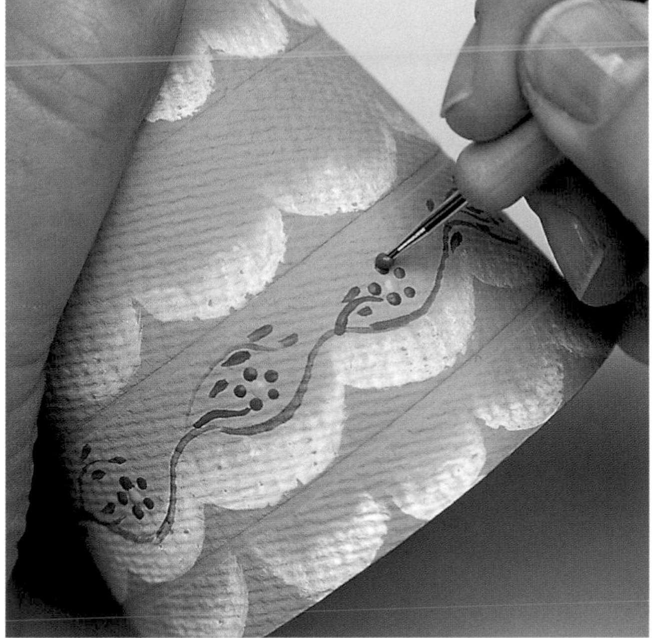

With your stylus and Rose Mist, make a circle of five dots for your flower. Add one dot in the center with your stylus and Straw to complete the blossom.

11 Shade the Hands

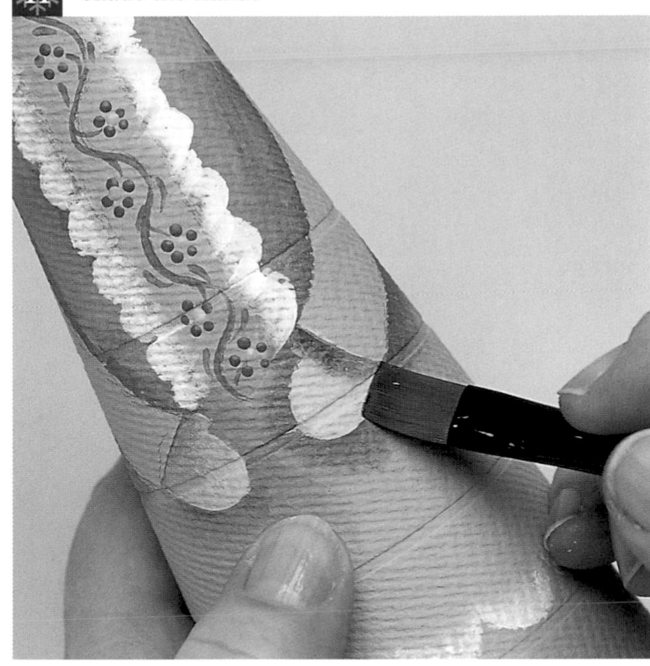

Corner-load your no. 10 flat with Burnt Sienna and shade the hands.

12 Add Cuffs to the Dress

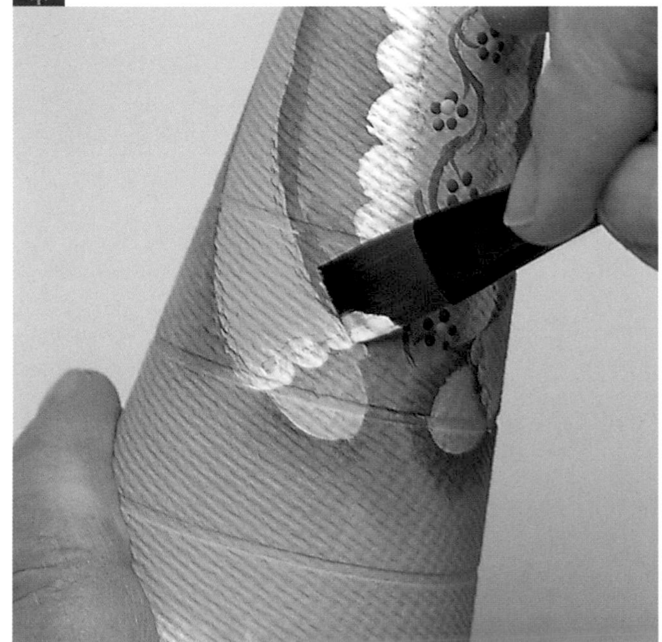

Using your no. 10 flat and White, float the ruffles on the hands.

13 Assemble the Angel

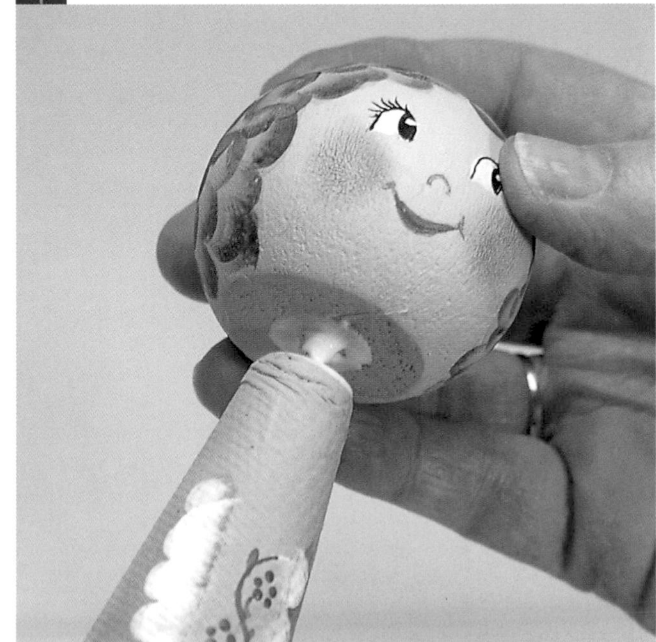

Add a dot of glue and assemble the angel.

14 Add the Rose in Her Hands

Add a dot of glue to the back of the flower, and place it between her hands.

15 Add Halo

Cut a small piece of the gold pipe cleaner and bend it into a circle to make a halo. Add a dot of glue, and place halo on her head.

16 Add Angel's Collar

Gather the lace and tie the ribbon around her neck. Trim any excess.

17 Glue on the Bow

Tie the pink ribbon in a bow. Add a dot of glue to the back of the ribbon and place on the lace collar, under the chin.

18 Add Angel's Wings

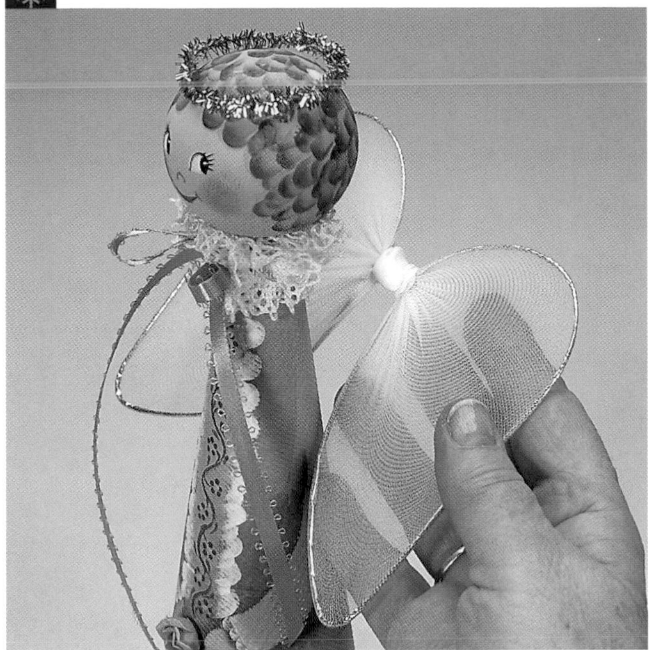

Add a dot of glue to the center of the wings, and press it into place on the back of the angel.

To protect the Gossamer Winged Angel, seal the face and body with two coats of water-based varnish.

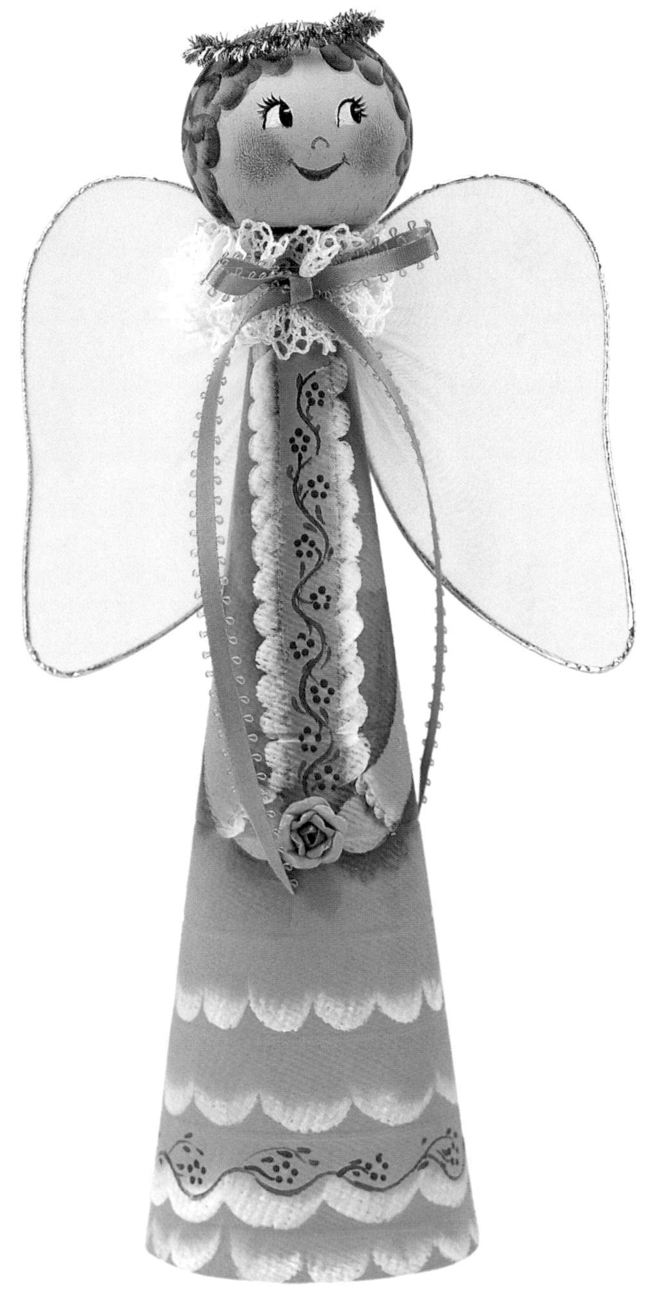

NOEL

NOEL PLAQUE

This is a festive design. It is painted on a slate plaque, which can hang on the wall, but this design would look great on any wood or fabric surface. The letters are made out of various holiday candy. Enjoy painting this fun project, and proudly display it in your home. It is sure to bring smiles to those who visit your house for the holidays!

materials:

11" (28cm) oval slate

Water-based varnish

Black and white graphite transfer paper

Stylus

Palette knife

*

BRUSHES

⅜-inch (10mm) angle

½-inch (12mm) angle

no. 10 flat

no. 8 flat

no. 3 round

10/0 liner

DELTA CERAMCOAT ACRYLIC PAINT

Green Isle

Opaque Red

Paynes Grey

White

Enlarge or reduce this template to fit your project.

1 Transfer Pattern

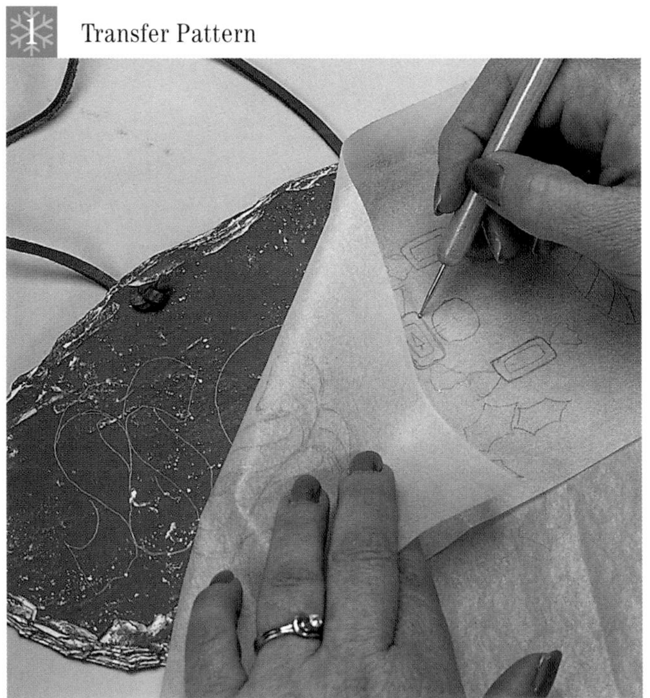

Apply pattern with white graphite transfer paper and your stylus.

2 Basecoat in White

With your no. 10 flat and White paint, basecoat each letter. When doing the "N", paint each section of the ribbon separately. This will probably take two to three coats of paint. When this is dry, reapply the detail lines of your pattern to each candy. Use black graphite transfer paper and your stylus.

3 Detail With Red

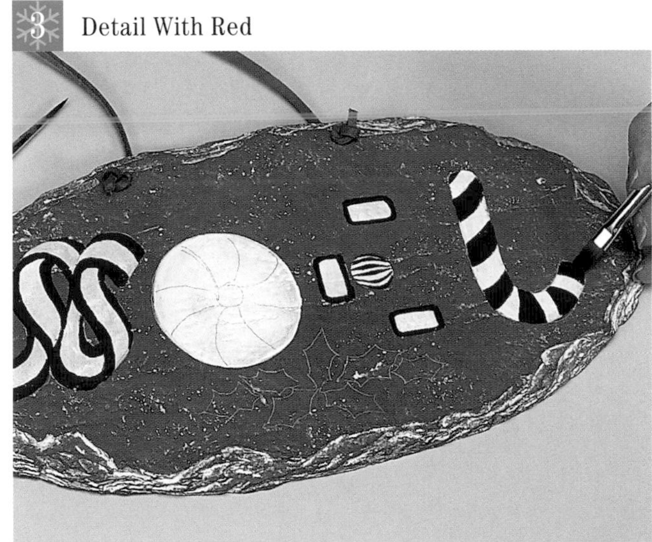

Use your no. 3 round brush and Opaque Red to add the red stripes to the letters. On the "E", the stripes on the ball candy should be wider in the center. To do this, start with light touch with your no. 3 round brush, press down harder in the center and then lift for a light touch to finish. For the "L", use your no. 8 flat to paint the stripes.

4 Detail With Green

Using your no. 3 round brush and Green Isle, add the green stripes, the green trees and the holly. With your no. 8 flat, paint in the green sections on the "O".

5 Shade the "N"

Using your ½-inch (12mm) angle and Paynes Grey, float along each section of the "N", giving it dimension. When this is dry, float across the folds of the candy.

6 Shade the "O"

With Paynes Grey and your ½-inch (12mm) angle, float the left side of the "O" and the right side of the center circle.

7 Shade the "E"

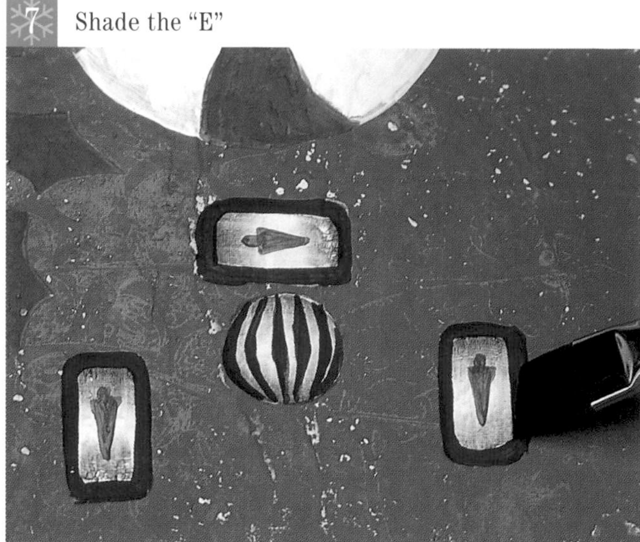

Corner-load Paynes Grey and your ½-inch (12mm) angle, float across the short ends of the tree candy. Float along the top and bottom of the ball candy.

8 Shade the "L"

With your ⅜-inch (10mm) angle and Paynes Grey, float along the outer edges. You will need to do this in two steps. Float one side, let it dry, and then do the other side.

9 Add the Wrapper Ends

Using your ⅜-inch (10mm) angle and White, corner-load your brush and paint the wrapper ends.

10 Paint On the Candy Wrappers

Using your no. 8 flat, make a wash with White paint, and brush over the tree candy. This needs to be sheer so it looks like cellophane.

11 Connect Wrappers to the Candy

Using your ⅜-inch (10mm) angle and White, corner-load your brush. Using the chisel edge of the brush, paint lines in the base of the wrapper ends so it looks like the paper is gathered and connected to the candy.

12 Paint Ties on Wrappers

With your 10/0 liner and Green Isle, paint ties on each end of the tree candies.

13 Highlight the "N" and "O"

With your 10/0 liner and White paint, add shine lines on the top two folds of the ribbon candy, as well as across the ribbon end. On the "O", run a line around the center.

14 Highlight the "E" and "L"

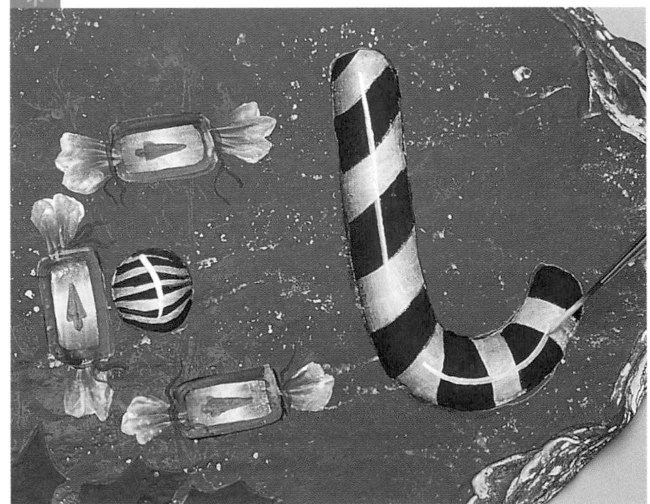

Using your 10/0 liner and White, make a curved line through the center of the ball candy. On the "L", highlight down the center.

15 Highlight the Holly

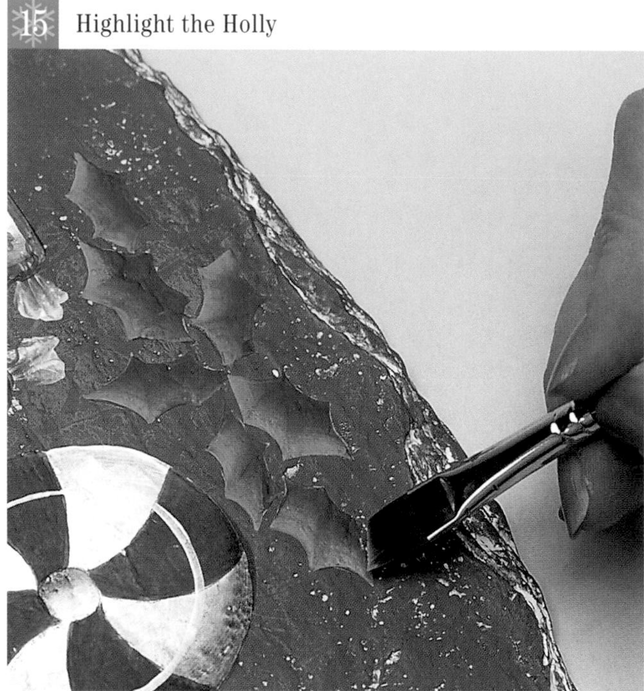

Using a palette knife, mix equal parts of Green Isle and White. With a ⅜-inch (10mm) angle, float the top side of each holly leaf.

16 Detail the Holly

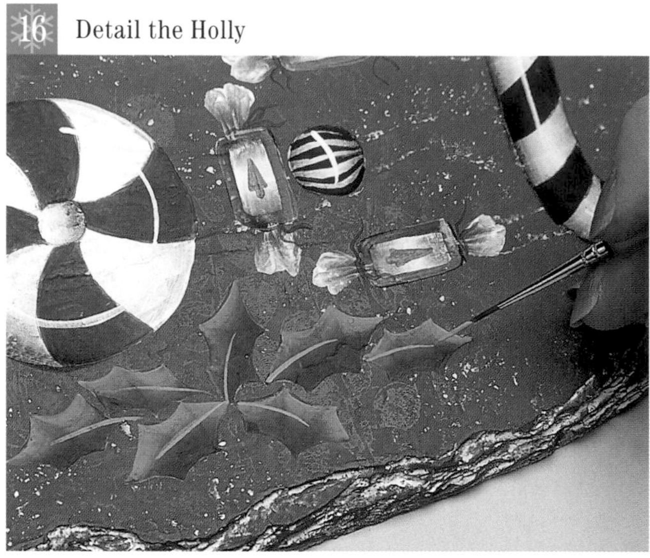

With the same light green mixture and your 10/0 liner, paint a vein in the center of each leaf.

17 Add the Berries

With the handle of a brush, paint berries with Opaque Red.

18 Highlight the Berries

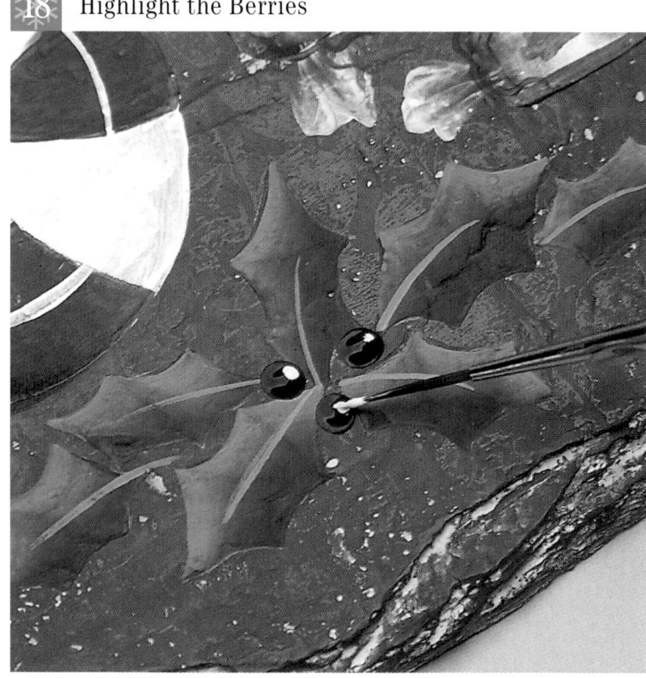

Using your 10/0 liner and White, place a highlight dot in each berry.

Finish the Noel Plaque with two coats of water-based varnish.

Catch me if you can

GINGERBREAD BOY ORNAMENT

Nothing revives childhood memories and Christmases past like the visions and aromas of gingerbread. This classic ornament is one you will always cherish. Whether you catch him or not doesn't really matter; he lives forever in the memory of a very special Christmas.

materials:

Star-shaped glass ornament
Frosted glass finish
Black graphite transfer paper
Stylus

⋆

BRUSHES

½-inch (12mm) flat
no. 8 flat
no. 2 liner
small Bobbi's Blender
no. 8 filbert

DELTA CERAMCOAT ACRYLIC PAINT

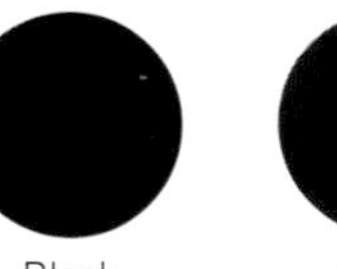

Black
Burnt Umber
Forest Green
Fruit Punch
Light Foliage Green
Light Ivory
Mocha Brown
Palomino Tan
Seminole Green

Enlarge or reduce this template to fit your project.

1 Prepare the Ornament for Painting

Wash and dry the ornament. Spray with the frosted glass finish. Allow it to dry according to the directions on the can. Transfer the pattern using black graphite transfer paper and your stylus.

2 Block In the Colors

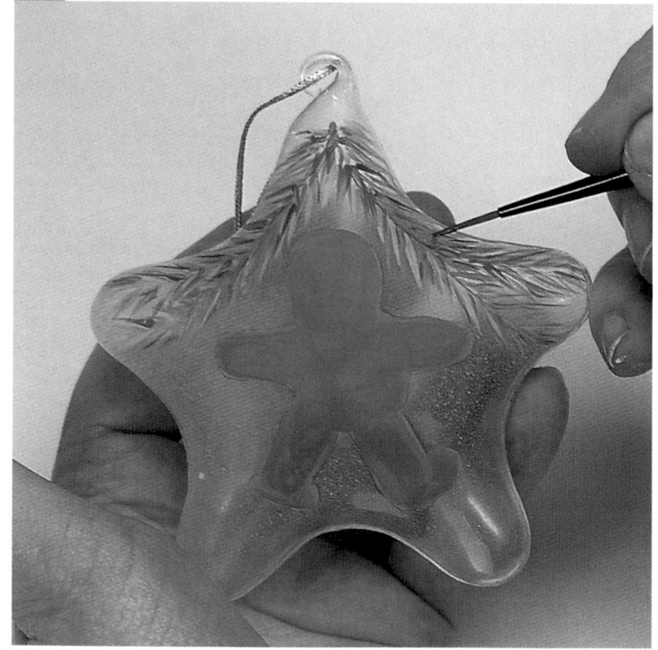

Using your no. 8 filbert, basecoat the entire gingerbread boy with Mocha Brown. Add the pine needles with your no. 2 liner and Light Foliage Green. Place the stem line in first and then pull the needles from the stem. Continue adding needles, first with Seminole Green and then with Forest Green. When finished, you will have three different colors of pine needles.

3 Shade the Gingerbread Man

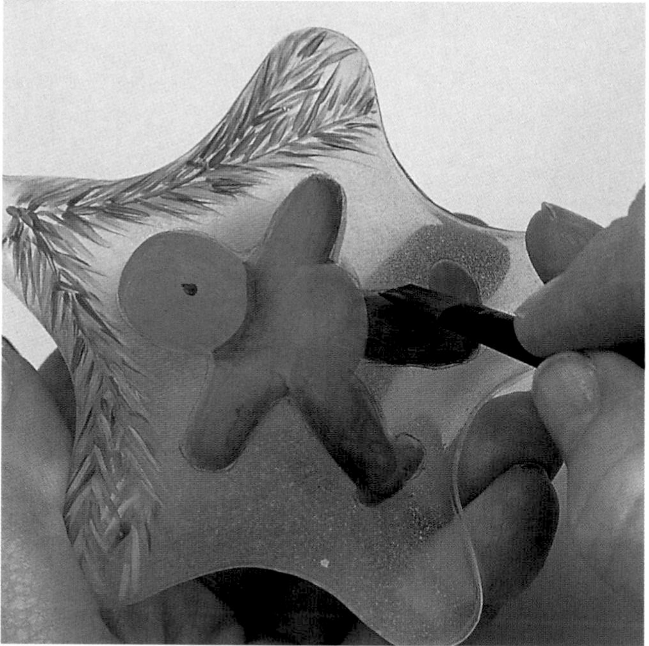

Corner-load your no. 8 flat, and float Burnt Umber under the chin, the arms, the body and the back of the legs.

4 Highlight the Body

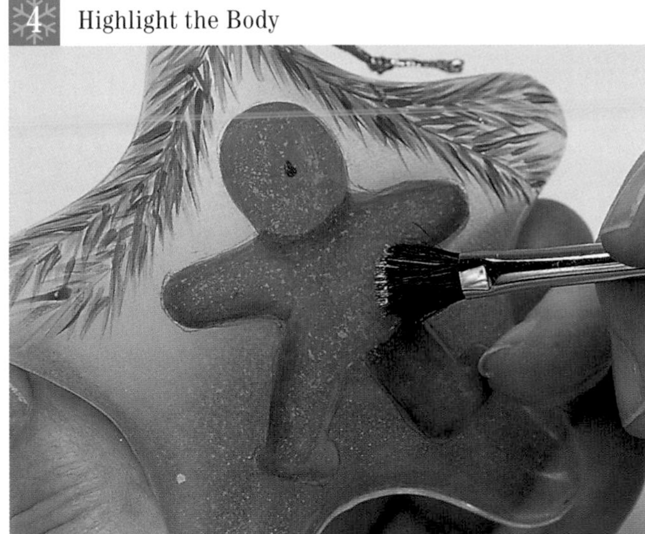

Using your small Bobbi's Blender mop, stipple the entire gingerbread boy with Palomino Tan.

5 Detail the Gingerbread Boy

Using the small end of your stylus and Black, add the eyes and nose. Add a smile with Fruit Punch and your no. 2 liner. With Fruit Punch paint and your stylus, finish with heart buttons. To make the hearts, use your stylus and place two dots side by side (they should barely touch). Gently pull the color down to a point to form hearts.

6 Add Icing Trim

With your no. 2 liner and Light Ivory, place a highlight in each eye at two o'clock. Continue using your no. 2 liner, and add a wavy line all the way around the gingerbread boy to represent icing.

Finish the Gingerbread Boy Ornament by floating Burnt Umber with your ½" (12mm) flat, so it looks like he is walking on the ground. Then add a message in black with your no. 2 liner.

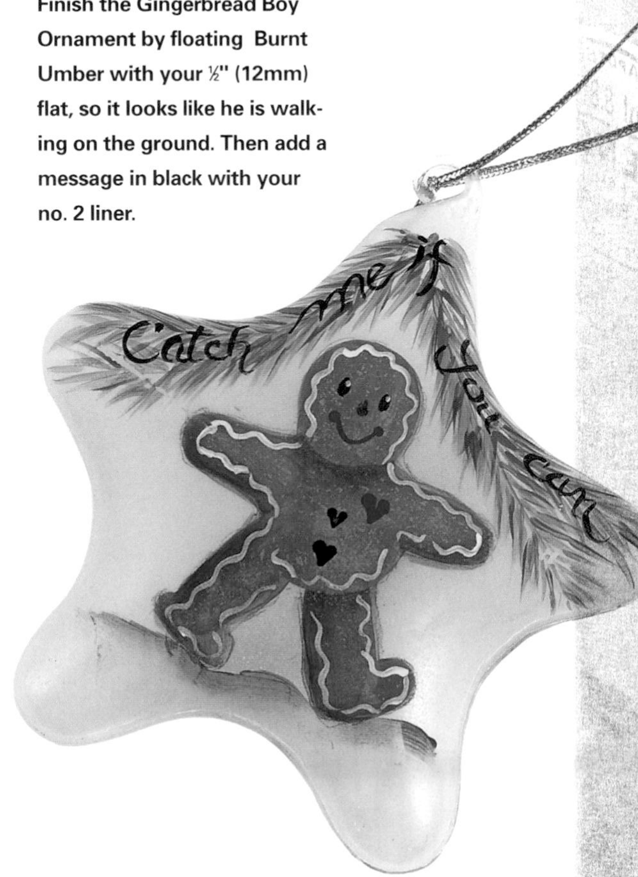

APOTHECARY
ml 8.8fl.oz
ENDER

SNOW DAY POT

Remember playing in the snow when you were little? You would spend the whole day making snowmen and snow angels and, of course, having snowball fights. Then you would come inside and warm up with hot chocolate. This piece will allow you to relive those fond memories all winter long.

materials:

4" (10cm) diameter clay pot

Saucer to fit for lid

Wooden snowman finial

Water-based varnish

Craft glue

Black and white graphite transfer paper

Stylus

Palette knife

*

BRUSHES

½-inch (12mm) angle

¾-inch (19mm) flat

no. 12 flat

no. 8 flat

no. 6 flat

no. 6 round

no. 1 liner

no. 4 fan

no. 6 sable

no. 4 scrubber

DELTA CERAMCOAT ACRYLIC PAINT

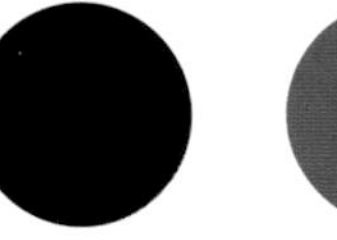

Black

Bungalow Blue

Cadet Blue

Coastline Blue

Custard

Dark Victorian Teal

Deep Lilac

Light Victorian Teal

Medium Flesh

Medium Victorian Teal

White

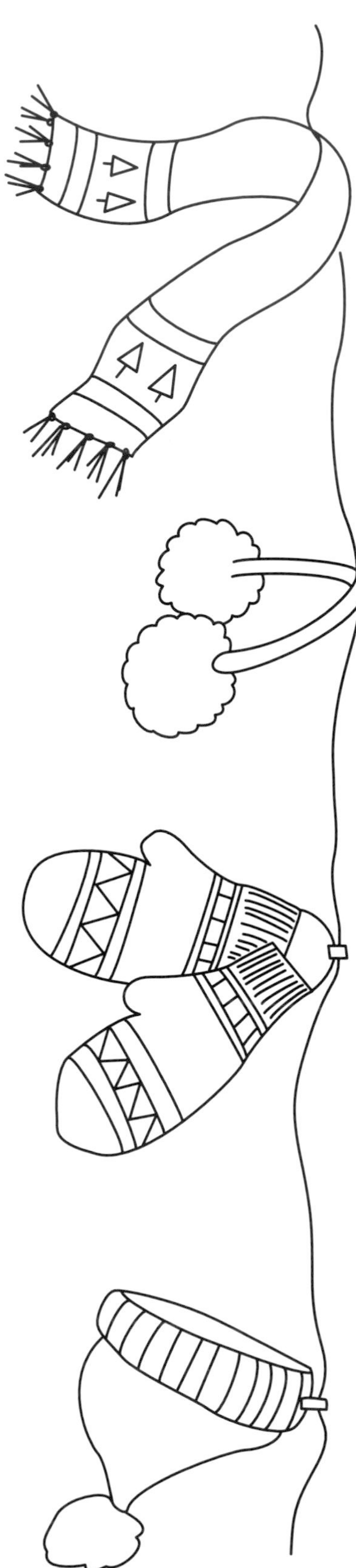

Enlarge or reduce this template to fit your project.

1 Basecoat the Pot

Basecoat the pot and the lid, inside and out, with Cadet Blue, using your ¾-inch (19mm) flat brush. With your no. 12 flat brush, basecoat the rim using Medium Victorian Teal. The snowman is done in White. When the paint is dry, apply the pattern with white graphite transfer paper and your stylus.

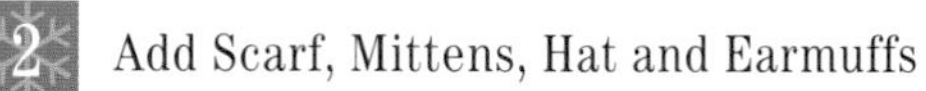

2 Add Scarf, Mittens, Hat and Earmuffs

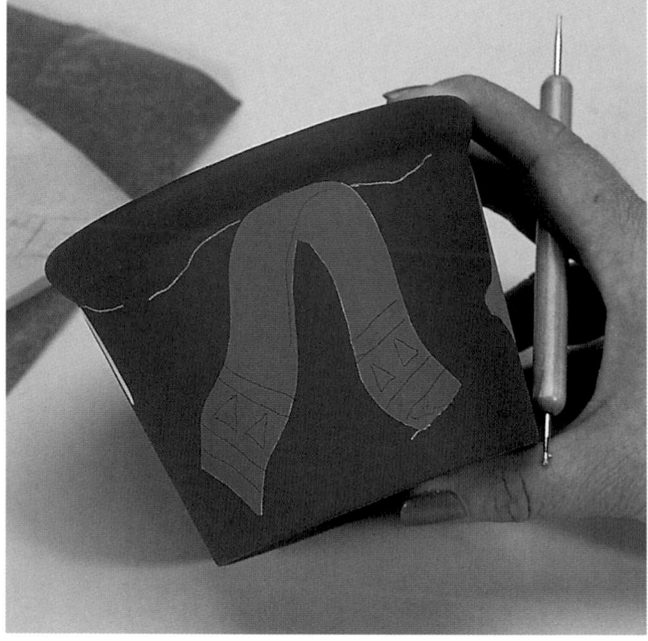

Using your no. 12 flat, paint the hat Medium Victorian Teal, the hatband Light Victorian Teal, inside the hatband Dark Victorian Teal, the scarf Bungalow Blue and the mittens Coastline Blue. With your no. 6 flat and Custard, paint the headband on your earmuffs. When your paint is dry, reapply the detail lines with black graphite transfer paper and your stylus.

3 Add Scarf Detail

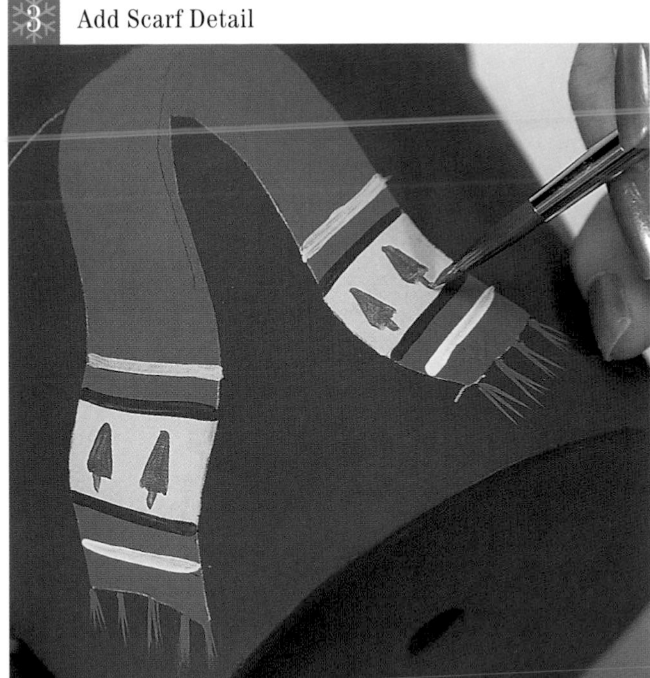

With your no. 8 flat, paint a stripe of Coastline Blue toward the bottom of each end. On either side, paint a stripe of Deep Lilac, using your no. 1 liner. Above the Deep Lilac, paint a stripe of Coastline Blue, and below the lower Deep Lilac stripe, paint a final stripe of Custard. The fringe is done in Bungalow Blue with your no. 1 liner. With your no. 6 round, paint trees on the large stripe in Dark Victorian Teal.

4 Shade the Scarf

Corner-load your ½-inch (12mm) angle with Cadet Blue, and shade the scarf. When this is dry, float across the fold of the scarf.

5 Highlight the Scarf

With your no. 4 round scrubber and White, scrub a highlight in the center sections of the scarf.

6 Detail the Fringe

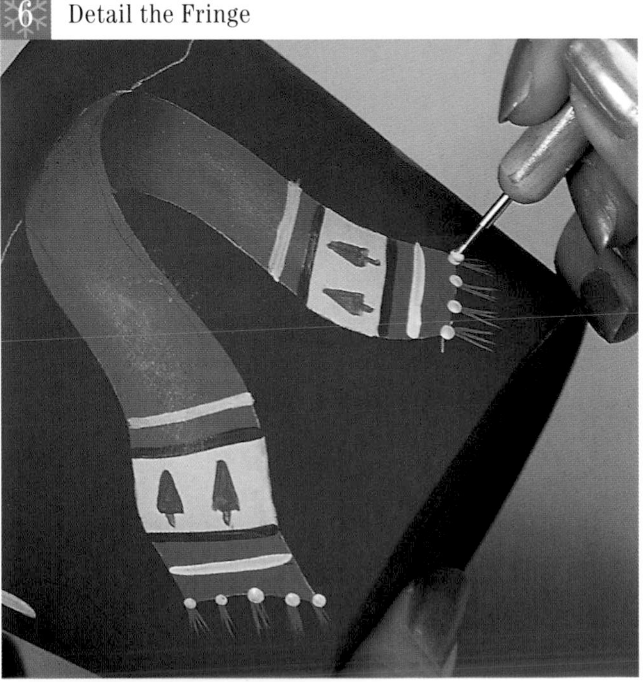

With your stylus, apply a Coastline Blue dot to the top of each fringe.

7 Detail the Hat

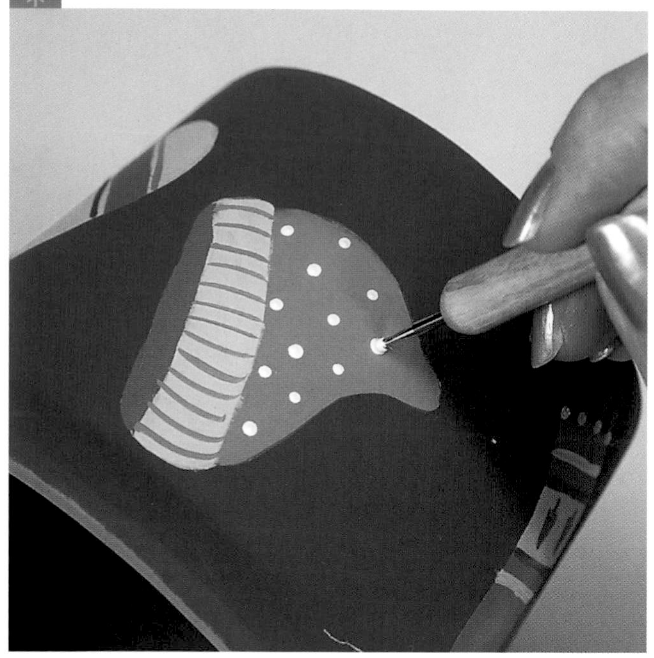

On the outside of the hatband, paint stripes of Medium Victorian Teal with your no. 1 liner. Add Custard dots to the body of the hat with your stylus.

8 Shade the Hat

With a ½-inch (12mm) angle and Dark Victorian Teal, float on the hat next to the hatband and along the outside edge of the hatband vertically.

9 Highlight the Hat

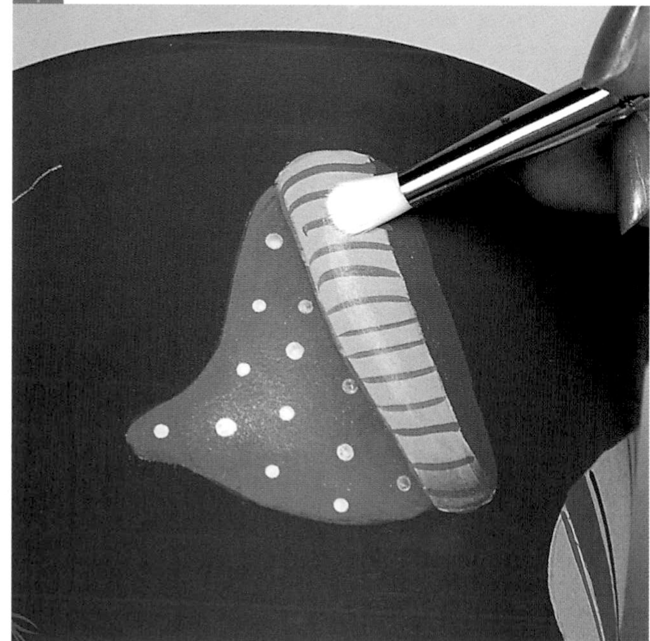

With your scrubber brush and White, scrub a highlight in the center of the body of the hat. Then, scrub a highlight horizontally on the hatband.

10 Add the Pom-Pom

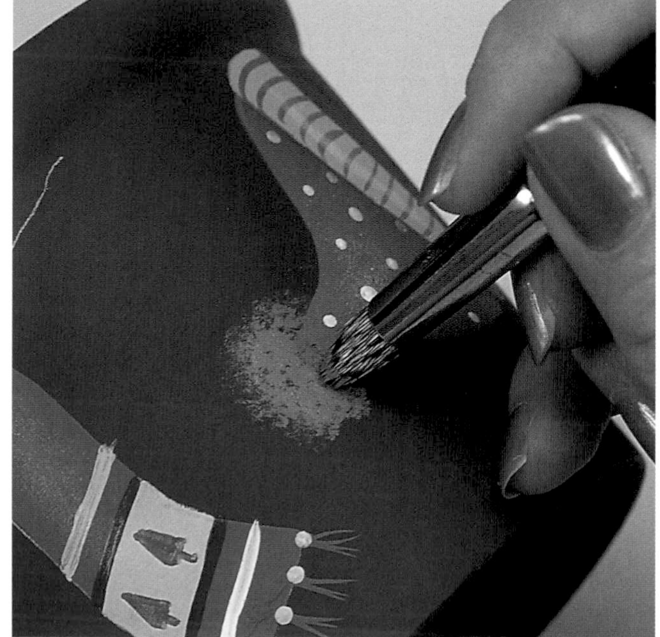

Using your no. 6 sable brush and Medium Victorian Teal, pounce a pom-pom on your hat.

11 Highlight the Pom-Pom

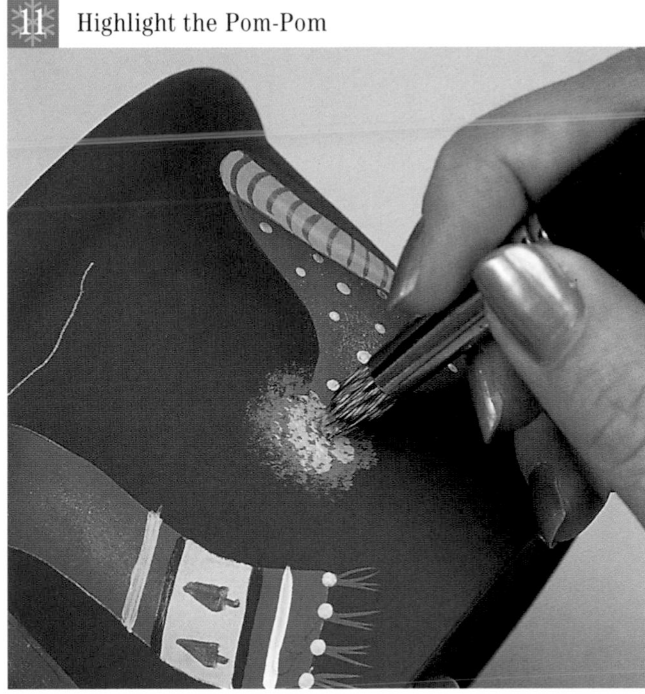

With your dirty sable brush, pick up a little Light Victorian Teal and pounce this in the center of your pom-pom.

12 Detail the Mittens

With your no. 6 flat and Bungalow Blue, paint a stripe across the mitten, and with your no. 6 round, place a slightly thinner Custard stripe above it. With your no. 1 liner, outline the Custard stripe with Medium Victorian Teal. Outline the Bungalow Blue stripe with a Medium Victorian Teal stripe on the bottom and a Deep Lilac one across the top of it. The rick rack on the Bungalow Blue stripe is done in Custard with your liner.

13 Continue Detail

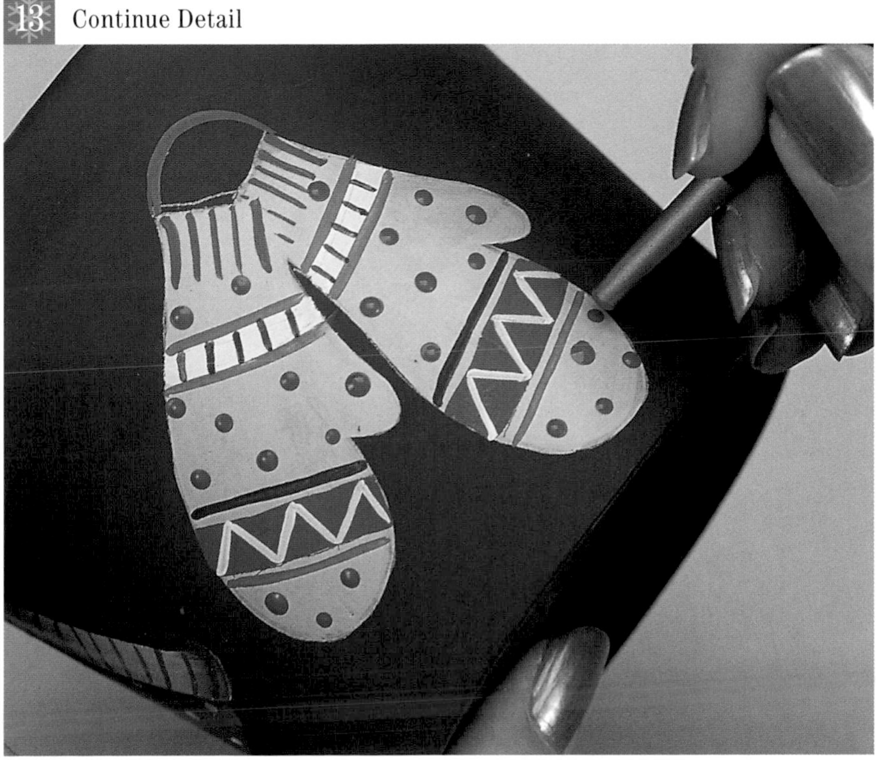

Add bars on the Custard stripe in Deep Lilac with your no. 1 liner. Then add vertical lines on the cuff with Bungalow Blue, which creates the effect of elastic ribbing. Use your liner and Bungalow Blue to paint the string connecting the mittens. Finally, with the handle of a brush, paint Bungalow Blue dots over the mittens.

14 Shade the Mittens

Corner-load your ½-inch (12mm) angle with Bungalow Blue, and float down the left side of both mittens.

15 Highlight the Mittens

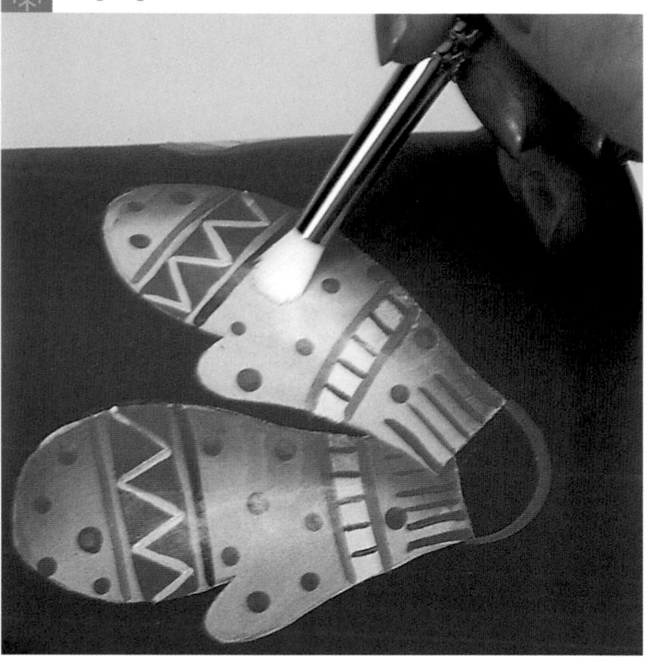

With your scrubber brush and White, scrub a highlight down the center of each mitten.

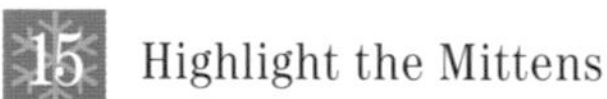

16 Shade the Headband

Shade the band with a ½-inch (12mm) angle and Bungalow Blue. Float across the bend of the earmuff.

17 Create the Earmuffs

With the sable brush and Deep Lilac, pounce in the earmuffs.

18 Highlight the Earmuffs

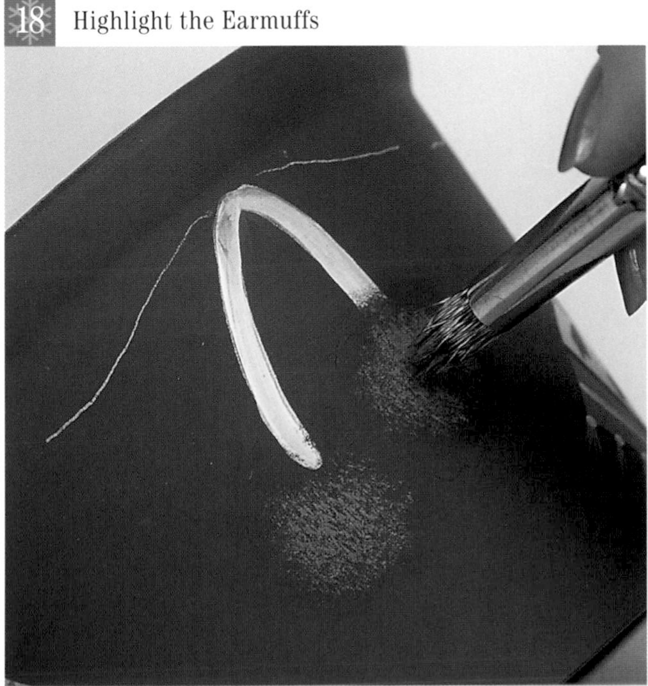

With the dirty sable brush, pick up a little bit of White and pounce in the center to highlight the earmuffs.

19 Highlight the Band

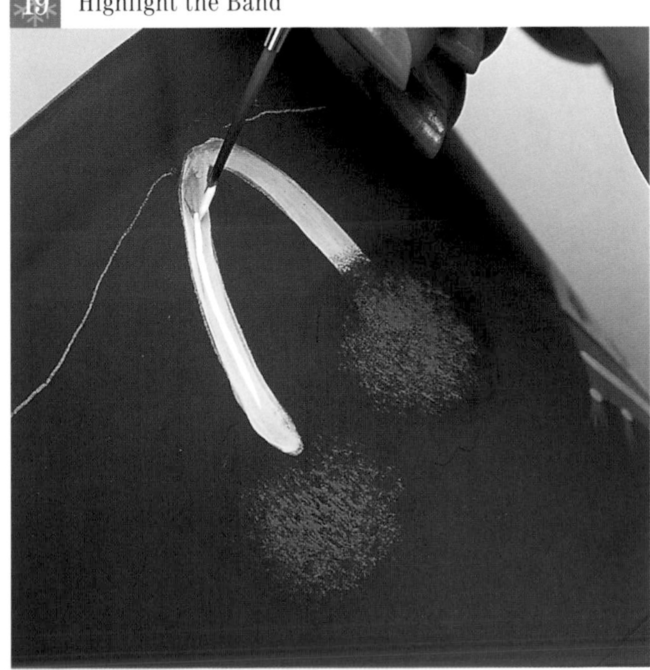

With your no. 1 liner, pick up White and place a line down the center of the headband.

20 Paint the Clothesline

Paint the clothesline using White and your no. 1 liner. When you get to the hat, add a clothespin, attaching it to the line.

21 Detail the Lid

With your no. 8 flat and Custard, paint a stripe around your lid. You will probably need two to three coats. Above the Custard line, use your no. 1 liner to apply a thin, wavy line with Medium Victorian Teal. Then, with the handle of your brush, apply Deep Lilac dots under the Custard stripe.

22 Detail the Snowman

With your no. 6 round and Bungalow Blue, paint the scarf on your snowman. Add stripes with your liner and Coastline Blue. For the cheeks, use your scrubber and Deep Lilac. Using your liner and Black, add eyes, nose, buttons, a smile and branch arms.

23 Add Snow

To make it look like it is snowing, use your fan brush and a palette knife. With thinned White, load your fan brush and spatter the pot (the spattering technique is outlined on page 13).

To finish the Snow Day Pot, glue the snowman finial on the lid. When the paint is dry, seal with a water-based varnish.

MERRY CHRISTMAS

TREETOP SANTA

It doesn't matter if you are ten or one hundred and ten; Santa lives in the heart of us all. We all know of his magical qualities. This happy fellow is a delight to make and to have. Perch him on top of the tree, or surround him with greens for a great centerpiece.

materials:

2 12" x 18" (30cm x 46cm) Sheets of 140-lb (300gsm) watercolor paper

Black string

Scissors

Glue stick

Sail needle

Black graphite transfer paper

Stylus

*

BRUSHES

¾-inch (19mm) flat

½-inch (12mm) flat

no. 4 flat

no. 1 liner

10/0 liner

medium Bobbi's Blender

no. 8 filbert

DELTA CERAMCOAT ACRYLIC PAINT

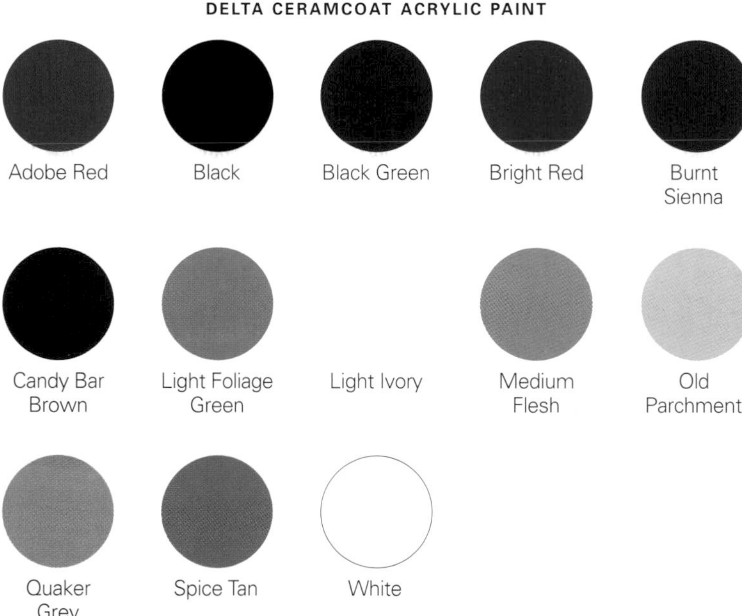

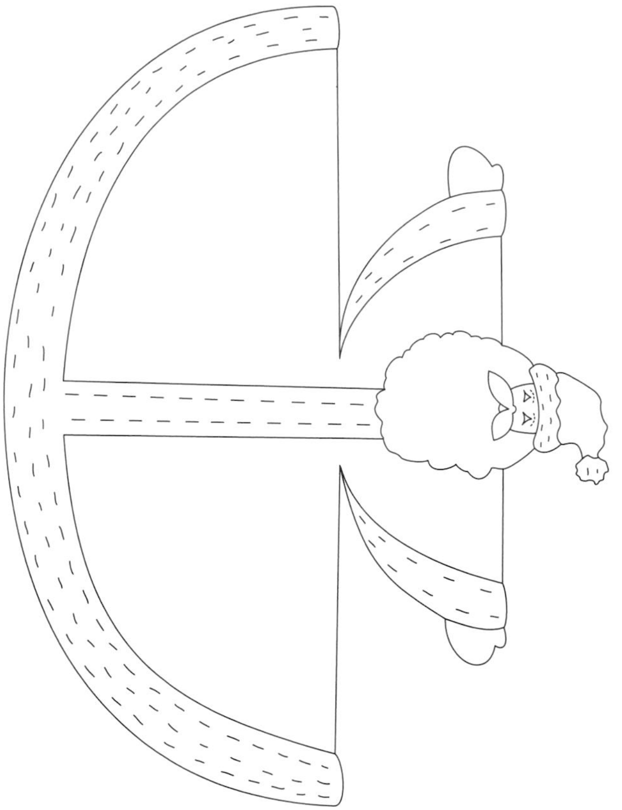

Enlarge or reduce this template to fit your project.

1 Apply Pattern and Basecoat

Transfer the major lines of the pattern. With your no. 8 filbert, basecoat the face in Medium Flesh; the hair, mustache and beard with Quaker Grey; and the mittens with Black Green. Using your ¾-inch (19mm) flat and Bright Red, base in the robe and hat. With your ½-inch (12mm) flat, basecoat the fur on the robe with Old Parchment. With the same color, basecoat the fur on the hat with your no. 8 filbert.

2 Add Facial Features

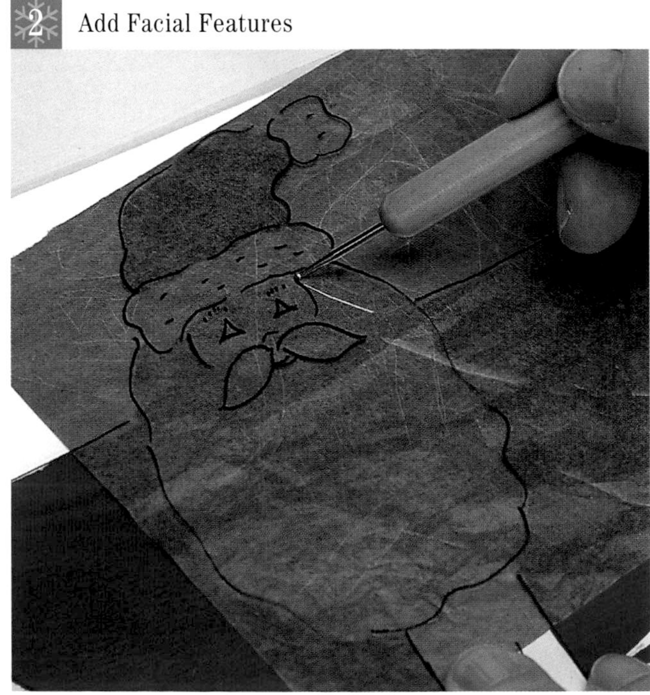

Transfer the pattern and add the facial features with your stylus and black graphite transfer paper.

3 Paint the Face

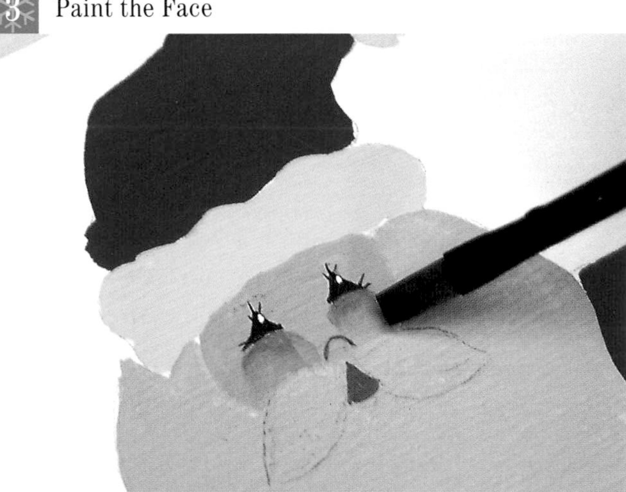

Using your 10/0 liner and Black, add the eyes and eyelashes. With the same brush, add a nose with Burnt Sienna and the mouth with Adobe Red. Continuing with your 10/0 liner, add a highlight in each eye with White at two o'clock. Switch to a no. 4 flat, and float on the cheeks with Adobe Red.

4 Add the Mustache and Beard

With your no. 1 liner, outline the mustache in White. Then, following the contour of the mustache, add additional lines. Use this same technique to do the beard. Start in the center of the beard and work out in both directions. After you have established the first layer of lines, add a second layer, and add a few curls near the end of the beard. Continue in this fashion until you have the amount of White that you would like. Add a few stokes of White coming out from under the hat onto the face.

5 Shade the Robe

Corner-load your ¾-inch (19mm) flat and Candy Bar Brown, shade around the fur on the robe. Float down the center on each side, along the top of the fur at the bottom, along the sleeves and around the beard. On the hat, float just above the fur trim and the pom.

HINT

Keep your Bobbi's Blender mop close by to soften any shading that may appear harsh.

6 Shade the Fur

Using your medium Bobbi's Blender and Spice Tan, stipple each side of the fur down the front, across the bottom, on the sleeves and on the hat. You will want a little of the Spice Tan to go onto the red for a more natural look.

7 Highlight the Fur

Using the same Bobbi's Blender, stipple Light Ivory down the center of the fur on the front, across the bottom, on the sleeves and on the hat.

8 Make It Ermine

Add Black dashes to the fur with your no. 1 liner. Randomly place these in all the fur areas.

9 Cut Out the Santa

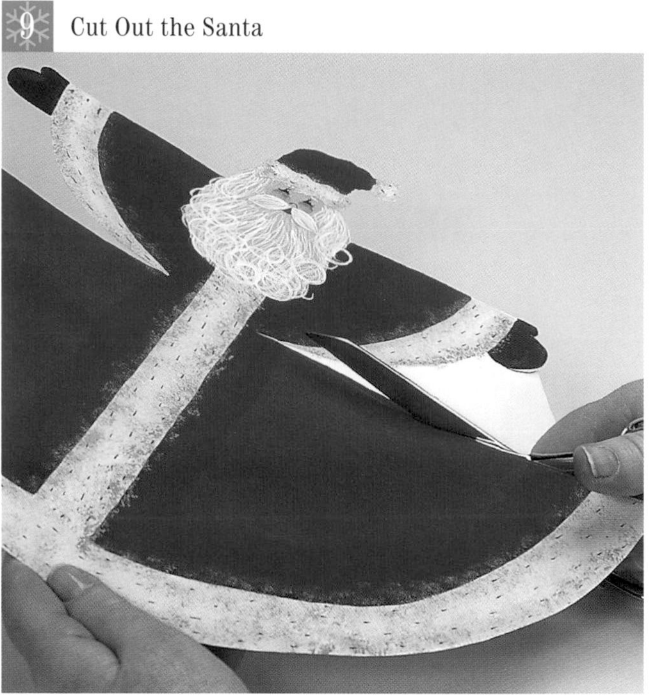

Using a sharp pair of scissors, cut out Santa.

10 Make Santa Stand Up

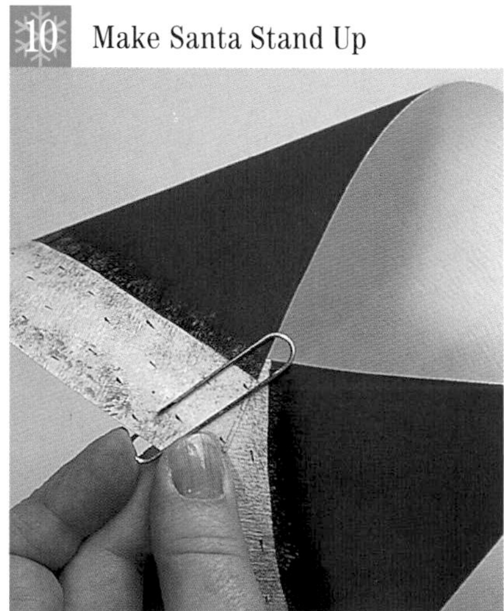

Take the edges of Santa's robe and curve him into a cone. Fasten the edges together with glue, a staple or a paper clip. If you use the paper clip, you will be able to lay him flat for storage and use throughout the years.

11 Make the Banner

Cut fourteen ¾-inch (2cm) squares of watercolor paper. Print "Merry Christmas" either by hand or by computer. Cut the letters into ½" (1cm) squares. Use a glue stick to glue the letters onto the watercolor paper squares.

12 Outline the Letters on the Banner

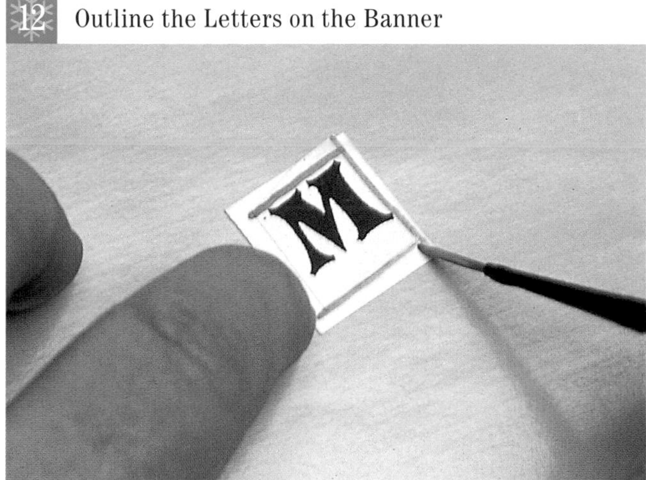

Using your no. 1 liner and Light Foliage Green, add a line all around the square to frame each letter.

13 String the Letters

Thread the sail needle and string the letters together to say Merry Christmas. Remember to string the letters starting with the last "S" in "Christmas".

Finish the Treetop Santa by tying the string so that the banner hangs along the edge of the sleeve line and across the middle of the Santa. Display on your treetop or as a centerpiece on your table.

SNOWMAN AND SNOWLADY TIN

This is a charming way to decorate any room. The snowman and snowlady invite a coziness to your home for the holidays. This project also has a practical side—it is a sturdy, galvanized tin container and can hold any number of items: Christmas cards, magazines, mittens or anything else you can think of!

materials

Oval galvanized tin
Metal primer
Water-based varnish
Black and white graphite transfer paper
Stylus
Palette knife

BRUSHES

½-inch (12mm) flat
no. 12 flat
no. 8 flat
no. 4 flat
no. 2 liner
no. 1 liner
medium Bobbi's Blender
no. 4 fan
1-inch (25mm) sponge

DELTA CERAMCOAT ACRYLIC PAINT

Black

Bright Red

Burnt Sienna

Candy Bar Brown

Dark Burnt Umber

Georgia Clay

Hunter Green

Light Ivory

Nightfall Blue

Pine Green

Quaker Grey

Tangerine

White

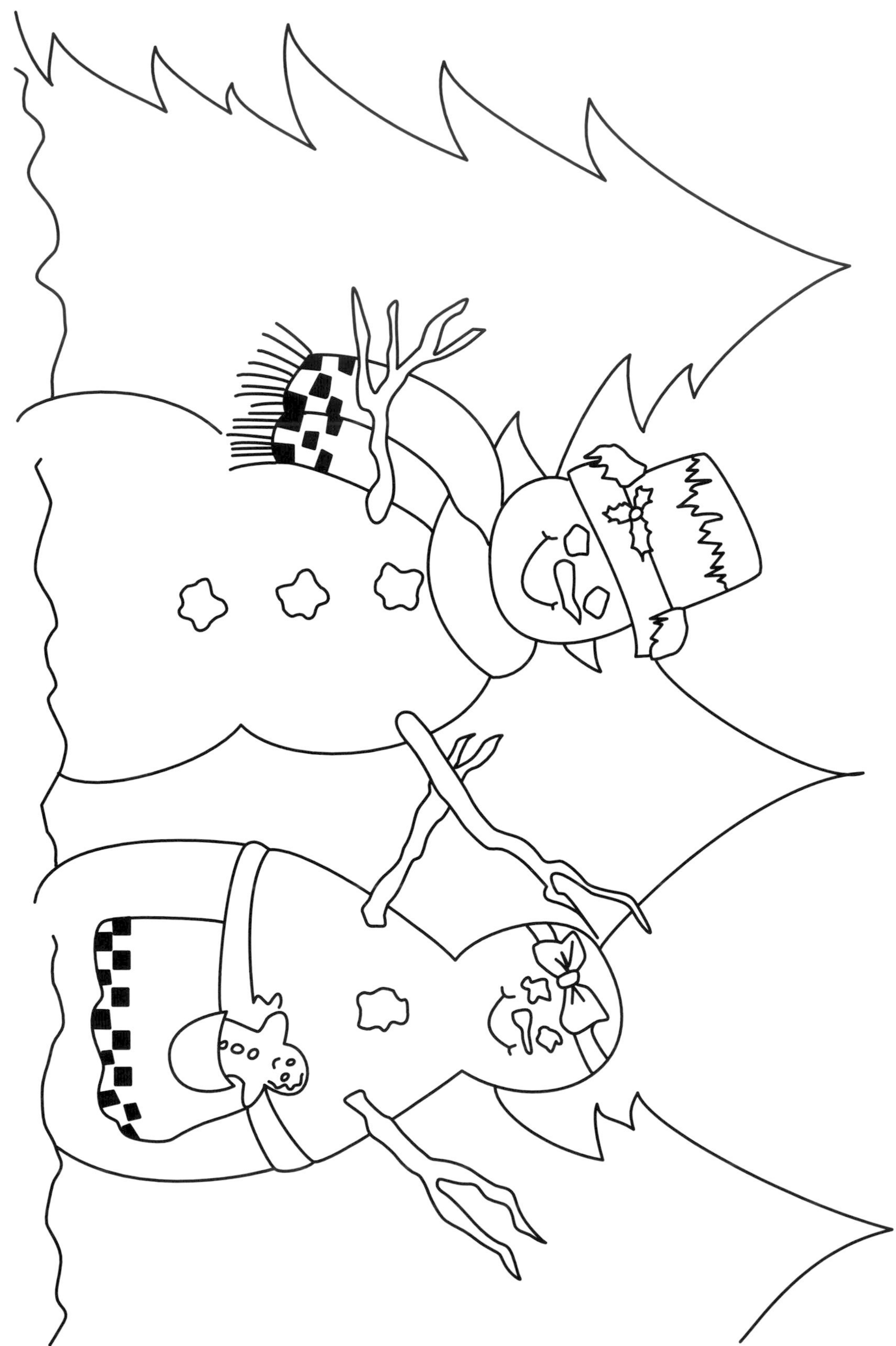

Enlarge or reduce this template to fit your project.

1 Prepare the Surface

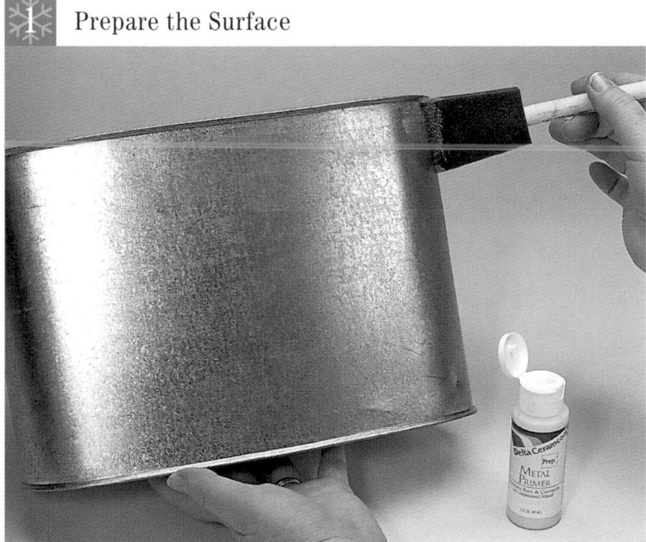

Clean the tin of any dust or debris, and brush on metal primer using your 1-inch (25mm) sponge brush. Allow it to dry before painting the surface.

2 Basecoat Background

Basecoat the entire tin with your 1-inch (25mm) sponge brush with Nightfall Blue. Apply the major lines of the pattern with white graphite transfer paper.

3 Add Background Trees

Using your medium Bobbi's Blender, stipple in the background trees with Pine Green.

4 Add Snow

Stipple snow on the limbs of the trees with White and your Bobbi's Blender.

5 Basecoat Snow Couple

Continue to use your medium Bobbi's Blender, and stipple in the snow couple with Quaker Grey.

6 Brighten Snow Couple

Stipple White paint on the snowman and snowlady. Keep the brightest area in the center.

7 Add Details to Snow Couple

On the snowman, use your no. 12 flat and paint his hat with Georgia Clay. Using the same brush, add his scarf and her apron with Bright Red. Switch to your no. 8 flat and add her headband.

8 Add More Details

Transfer the remainder of the pattern with black graphite transfer paper and your stylus.

9 Add the Facial Features and Buttons

Using your no. 4 flat, paint the noses with Tangerine, the eyes and buttons with Black and the gingerbread boy with Burnt Sienna. Use your no. 1 liner and paint smiles on both faces.

10 Shade the Snowman and Add Holly

Corner-load your ½-inch (12mm) flat with Candy Bar Brown and shade the scarf. Continuing with your ½-inch (12mm) flat, float a shade of Burnt Sienna along the rim of the hat. Using your no. 1 liner, basecoat the holly with Hunter Green. Take your stylus and add holly berries with Bright Red.

11 Shade the Apron and Bow

Corner-load your ½-inch (12mm) flat for floated color with Candy Bar Brown, and shade the apron. On the bow, shade each side of the knot, the tops of the front loops and on each side where it goes around the head.

12 Detail the Gingerbread Boy

Using your no. 2 liner and Black, add the facial features and the buttons. Continue with your no. 2 liner and Light Ivory, and put the icing trim all around the gingerbread boy.

13 Add the Clothing Trim

With your no. 2 liner and White, add the fringe to the bottom of each end of the scarf. Take your no. 4 flat and White, and add checks to each end of the scarf and to the bottom of the apron.

14 Add Twig Arms

Using your no. 2 liner and Dark Burnt Umber, add the twig arms to each snow person.

15 Add the Snow

Using your no. 2 liner, pick up a heavy load of White and dab on the twig arms and on the hat to represent snow. Keep this loose and uneven. Add a highlight on the left side of each button and in each eye with a dab of White.

16 Add Trim to the Top of the Tin

With your ½-inch (12mm) flat, load your brush and place the checks going around the top of the container.

17 Spatter the Tin

Load your fan brush with White. Tap gently on a paper towel to remove excess paint. Holding your palette knife in your other hand, gently tap the fan brush to make it "snow." When dry, seal with a water-based varnish. Note: If you do not have a palette knife, you may use the handle of another sturdy brush.

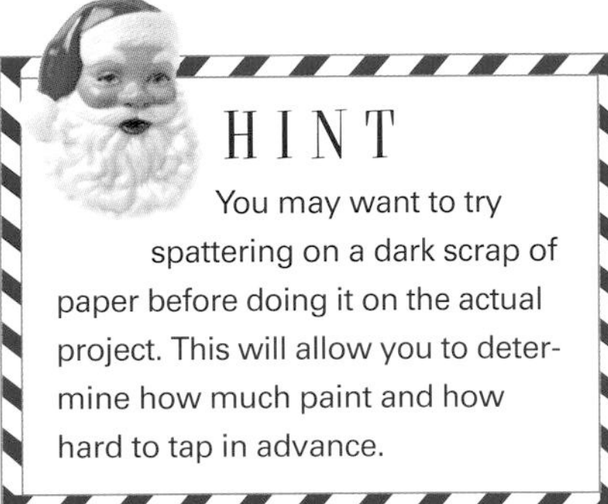

HINT

You may want to try spattering on a dark scrap of paper before doing it on the actual project. This will allow you to determine how much paint and how hard to tap in advance.

When the Snowman and Snowlady Tin is dry, seal with a water-based varnish.

ecilia
Nickolas
ebecca

JOY TRAY

Whether you are hearing Christmas carols of joy, the sound of bells joyfully ringing or the joyful laughter of children, Christmas is a time of joy. This Joy Tray can help bring the spirit of Christmas into your home. It can be used for its intended purpose of serving, or it could be used to decorate a mantel or shelf. You could also fill it with all sorts of cookies, cakes and candies and give it to a special friend.

materials

10" x 13" (25cm x 33cm) Wooden tray

All-purpose sealer

Water-based varnish

Medium- to fine-grade sandpaper

Black and white graphite transfer paper

Stylus

Palette knife

BRUSHES

½-inch (12mm) flat

no. 10 flat

no. 2 flat

no. 2 liner

small Bobbi's Blender

no. 6 fan

no. 8 filbert

2-inch (51mm) sponge brush

DELTA CERAMCOAT ACRYLIC PAINT

Antique White

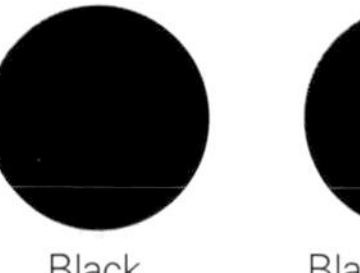

Black

Black Green

Burnt Umber

Candy Bar Brown

Dark Forest Green

Hunter Green

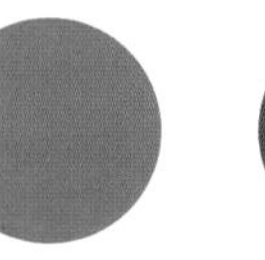

Light Foliage Green

Mocha Brown

Old Parchment

Perfect Highlight for Red

Pine Green

Raw Sienna

Tompte Red

White

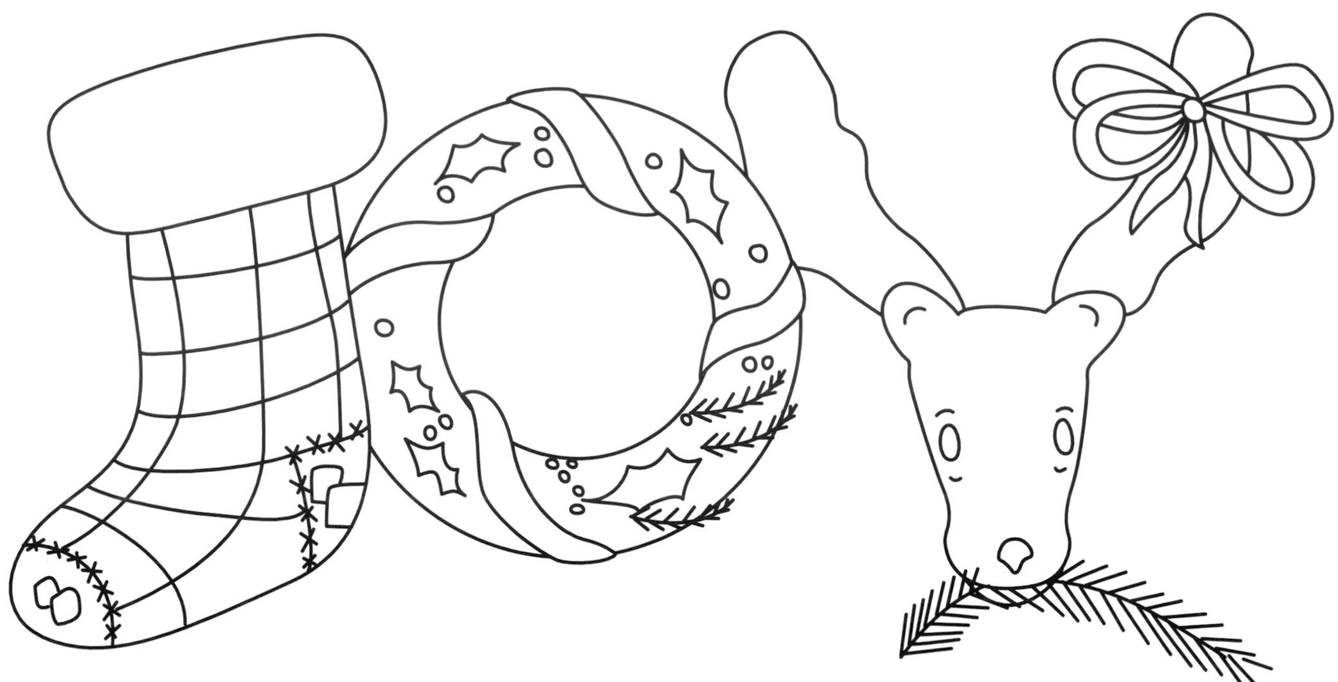

Enlarge or reduce this template to fit your project.

1 Prepare Surface to Paint

Sand and seal the tray as instructed in the Preparing Surfaces section on page 17. Lightly resand, if necessary. Using the 2-inch (51mm) sponge brush, basecoat the entire tray with Antique White. Transfer pattern with black graphite transfer paper and stylus.

2 Basecoat the J-O-Y

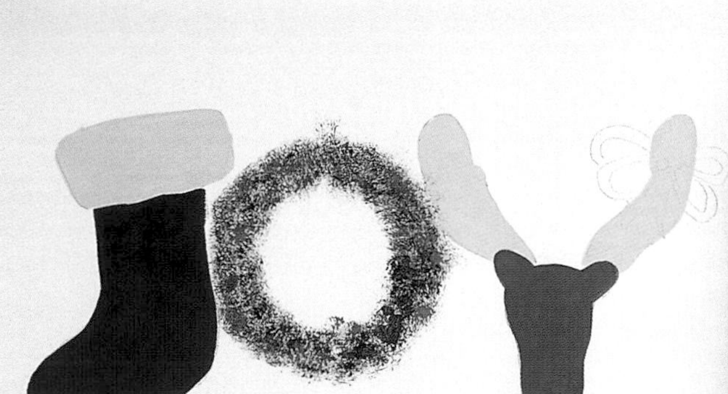

Basecoat the fur of the stocking using your ½-inch (12mm) flat and Old Parchment, and the rest of the stocking with Tompte Red. Use your Bobbi's Blender mop and Dark Forest Green, Black Green and Light Foliage Green to stipple in the wreath. Make sure all three colors show. Take your no. 8 filbert and basecoat the reindeer with Mocha Brown and his antlers with Old Parchment. Transfer the details from the pattern with white graphite transfer paper and stylus.

3 Add Details

With your no. 10 flat, basecoat the heel and the toe of the stocking with Raw Sienna. Basecoat the holly leaves with Hunter Green. Add the ribbon with Tompte Red. Basecoat the ribbon with equal parts of Tompte Red and White. This will prevent the wreath from showing through the ribbon.

HINT

By mixing equal parts of a color with White, you can paint over a dark color in the background and prevent the darker color from showing through.

4 Shade the Ribbon

Using your ½-inch (12mm) flat and Candy Bar Brown, float under the fur of the stocking and the edges of the ribbon where it appears to go behind the wreath. Using your no. 10 flat brush, float a highlight on each holly leaf with Light Foliage Green. Add veins with your no. 2 liner and Light Foliage Green.

5 Add Details to the Wreath and Stocking

Using your no. 2 liner, add some pine needles to the wreath with Pine Green. Keep them loose and flowing around the wreath. Next add details to the stocking. Apply the stripes with your no. 2 liner. First, put in the Old Parchment stripes, and then add the Hunter Green stripe to the right side of the Old Parchment stripes. Taking the small Bobbi's Blender mop, stipple both edges of the fur with Raw Sienna.

6 Highlight Fur

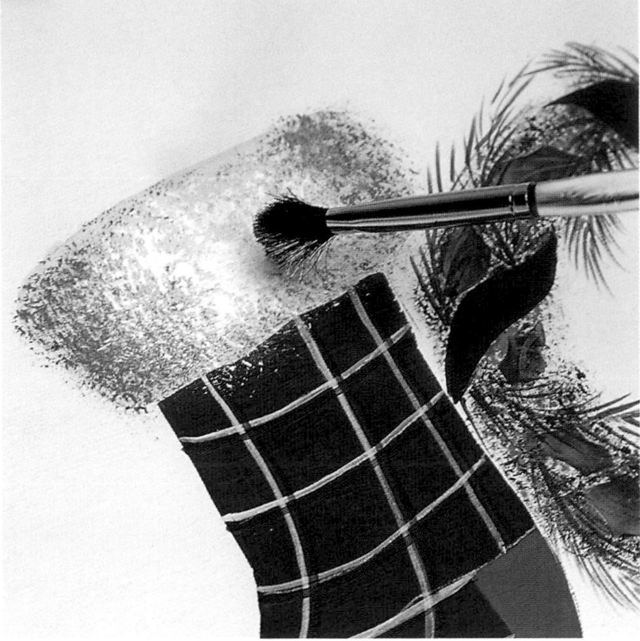

Stipple White in the center of the fur area with your Bobbi's Blender. Start in the middle of the fur, and soften as you go toward the edges.

7 Complete the Stocking

Shade under the fur and along the left side of the stocking by corner-loading your ½-inch (12mm) flat with Candy Bar Brown. With your no. 2 flat, add the patches to the heel and toe, first with Light Foliage Green and then with Dark Forest Green. Add the stitching with Black and your no. 2 liner.

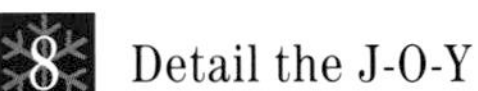

8 Detail the J-O-Y

Using Raw Sienna and your ½-inch (12mm) flat, float along each side of the fur on the stocking. Moving on to the wreath with the same brush, place a back-to-back float with Perfect Highlight for Red in the center of the ribbon. Using your no. 2 liner and Black, paint in the eyes, nose and mouth of the reindeer. With your ½-inch (12mm) flat and Black, float a C-stroke in each ear.

9 Shade and Highlight the Reindeer's Face

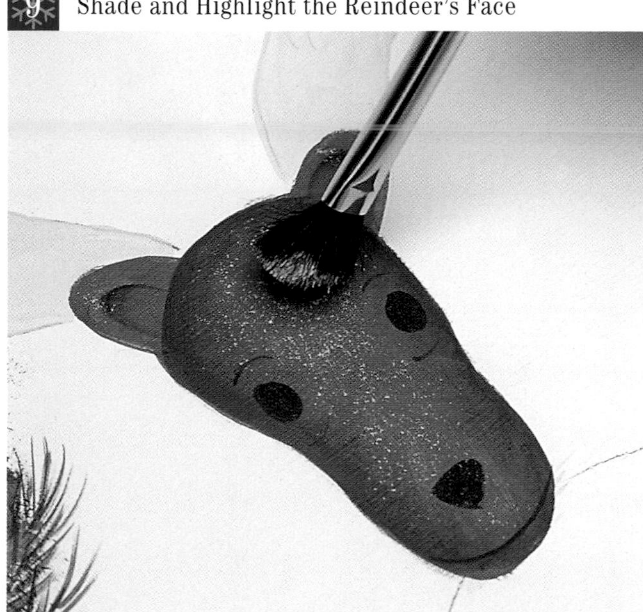

With Burnt Umber and your ½-inch (12mm) flat, float a shade all around the outer edge of the face. Stipple the entire face with the Bobbi's Blender and Old Parchment. Keep this rather light and soft. The brightest area should be in the center of the face.

10 Add Rosy Cheeks and a Twinkle in Reindeer's Eyes

Continue to use the Bobbi's Blender, and drybrush the cheeks with Tompte Red. Make sure the brush is dry with very little paint to keep this soft. Highlight the eyes and nose with White and the tip end of the no. 2 liner.

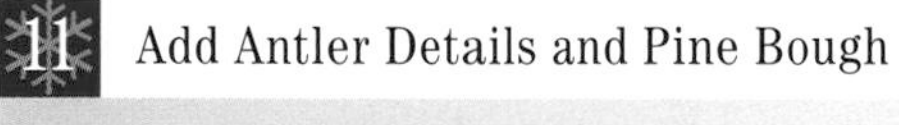

11 Add Antler Details and Pine Bough

Float a shade all around the antlers with your ½-inch (12mm) flat and Raw Sienna. Base in the ribbon the same as the ribbon in the wreath with your no. 2 liner. Shade and highlight the ribbon the same as the ribbon on the wreath using your no. 10 flat. Add the pine bough in the reindeer's mouth using your no. 2 liner and Hunter Green. To add dimension, add a few more pine needles with Black Green and your no. 2 liner.

12 Add Berries

Using the large end of your stylus, apply the berries with Tompte Red.

13 Add Checkerboard

Starting with one check in each corner and your ½-inch (12mm) flat brush, add the checks in each of the corners with Tompte Red.

14 Paint the Trim

With your 2-inch (51mm) sponge brush and Tompte Red, apply the trim to the edges of the tray.

15 Add Spattering

Spatter the entire tray using the fan brush, palette knife and Raw Sienna. (See the spattering technique on page 13 for more details.)

When the Joy Tray is dry, seal with three to four coats of a water-based varnish.

CHRISTMAS TREE CARD HOLDER

It's that time of year when we seem to receive more mail than ever, and not just any kind of letters, but special cards and keepsakes from friends and family. This Christmas Tree Card Holder is an ideal place to keep those important pieces of mail from loved ones. You can keep them under the tree until you get a chance to respond.

materials

13 ½" x 10" (34cm x 25cm) Wooden card holder (available at craft stores)

All-purpose sealer

Medium- to fine-grade sandpaper

Black and white graphite transfer paper

Stylus

Sea sponge

BRUSHES

⅝-inch (16mm) angle

⅜-inch (10mm) angle

¾-inch (19mm) flat

no. 12 flat

no. 8 flat

5/0 liner

no. 6 filbert

no. 6 round scrubber

DELTA CERAMCOAT ACRYLIC PAINT

Blue Lagoon

Dark Foliage Green

Light Foliage Green

Lime Green

Medium Foliage Green

Opaque Red

Paynes Grey

Perfect Highlight for Red

Straw

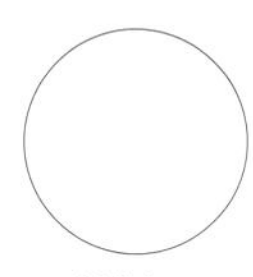
White

Enlarge or reduce this template to fit your project.

1 Basecoat the Tree

Sand, seal and resand the wood as outlined in the Preparing Surfaces section on page 17. Basecoat with Dark Foliage Green, using your ¾-inch (19mm) flat brush. Be sure to basecoat the entire piece of wood, including the inside of the box and the back side of the tree.

2 Create Tree Boughs, Part 1

Using a damp sea sponge and Medium Foliage Green, sponge all over the tree area.

3 Create Tree Boughs, Part 2

Without cleaning the sponge, pick up some Dark Foliage Green, and sponge over the tree area.

4 Create Tree Boughs, Part 3

Next, pick up some of the Light Foliage Green on a different edge of your sponge. Concentrate the Light Foliage Green at the top of your branches. When you are finished with these three steps, the entire tree should be covered and look three-dimensional.

5 Transfer Pattern

When your tree is dry, apply the pattern with white graphite transfer paper and your stylus. Use black graphite transfer paper on the gifts.

6 Define the Boughs

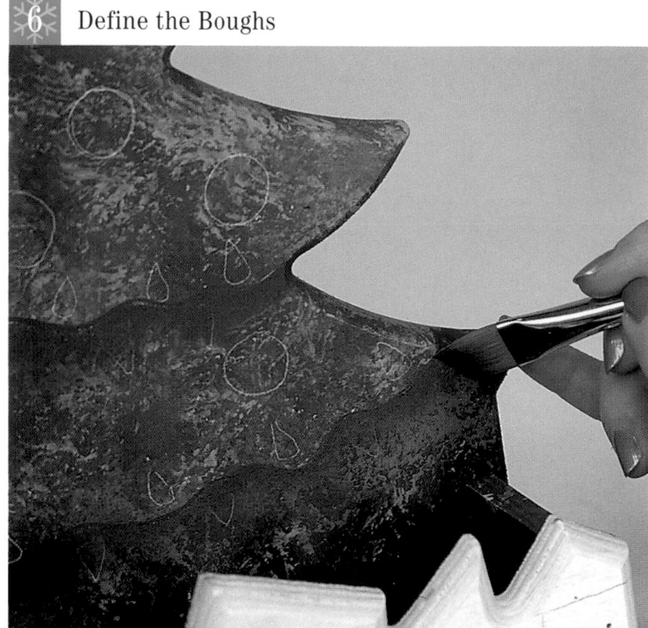

With your ⅝-inch (16mm) angle and Dark Foliage Green, float under the light strings.

7 Add the Light Cords

With Dark Foliage Green and your 5/0 liner, paint the light cords.

8 Highlight the Light Cords

While this is still wet, and with your dirty 5/0 liner, pick up some Light Foliage Green and highlight the light cord.

17 Add Final Details

With your 5/0 liner and White, paint shine marks on the left side of each light. Then, paint shine marks on each red ball ornament— a long shine mark at seven o'clock and a short shine mark at two o'clock. Add sparkles by painting a vertical line then a horizontal line and, finally, adding an X. Put a dot of White in the center with your stylus. Paint ornament hooks with Straw and your liner. Don't close them because they are hooked to the tree. To finish the piece, add a base to each of your lights and attach it to the string of lights. Use your liner and Paynes Grey. Place a short line under each light base.

When the Christmas Tree Card Holder is dry, seal with three to four coats of a water-based varnish.

TEMPLATE GALLERY

Here are more projects to inspire you and keep your creative juices flowing. Let your imagination take you away and add your own personal touch. You may want to experiment and apply these designs on a variety of mediums. Reduce or enlarge the templates as needed.

These adorable gifts are painted on magnetic sheeting, and add a festive touch to your refrigerator to proudly hang children's projects, holiday party invitations or Christmas cards from friends and family. Paint on canvas and they make charming coasters.

This pine and sleigh bell design is painted with acrylic paint after the ornament has been sprayed with frosted glass finish.

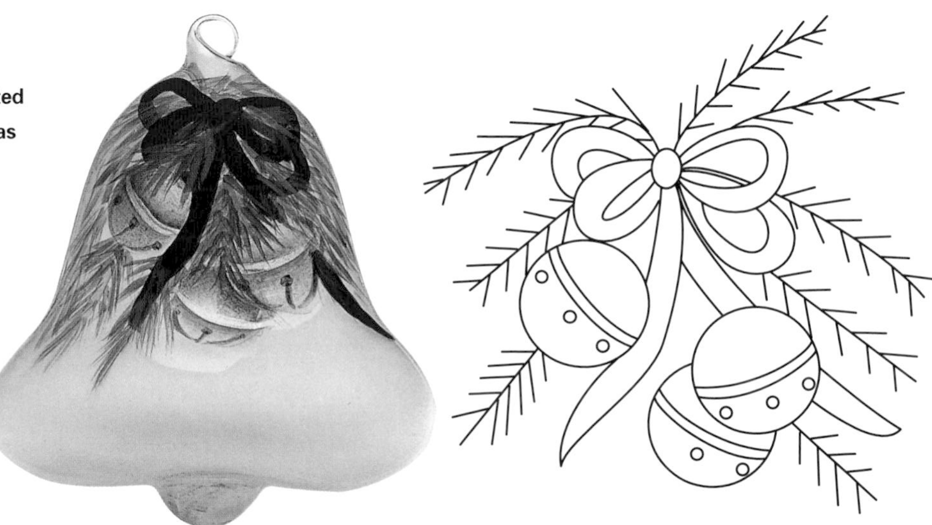

Proudly display Rudolph in your kitchen for the Christmas season. This reindeer potholder is an excellent complement to the Gingerbread Man Potholder and Child's Apron.

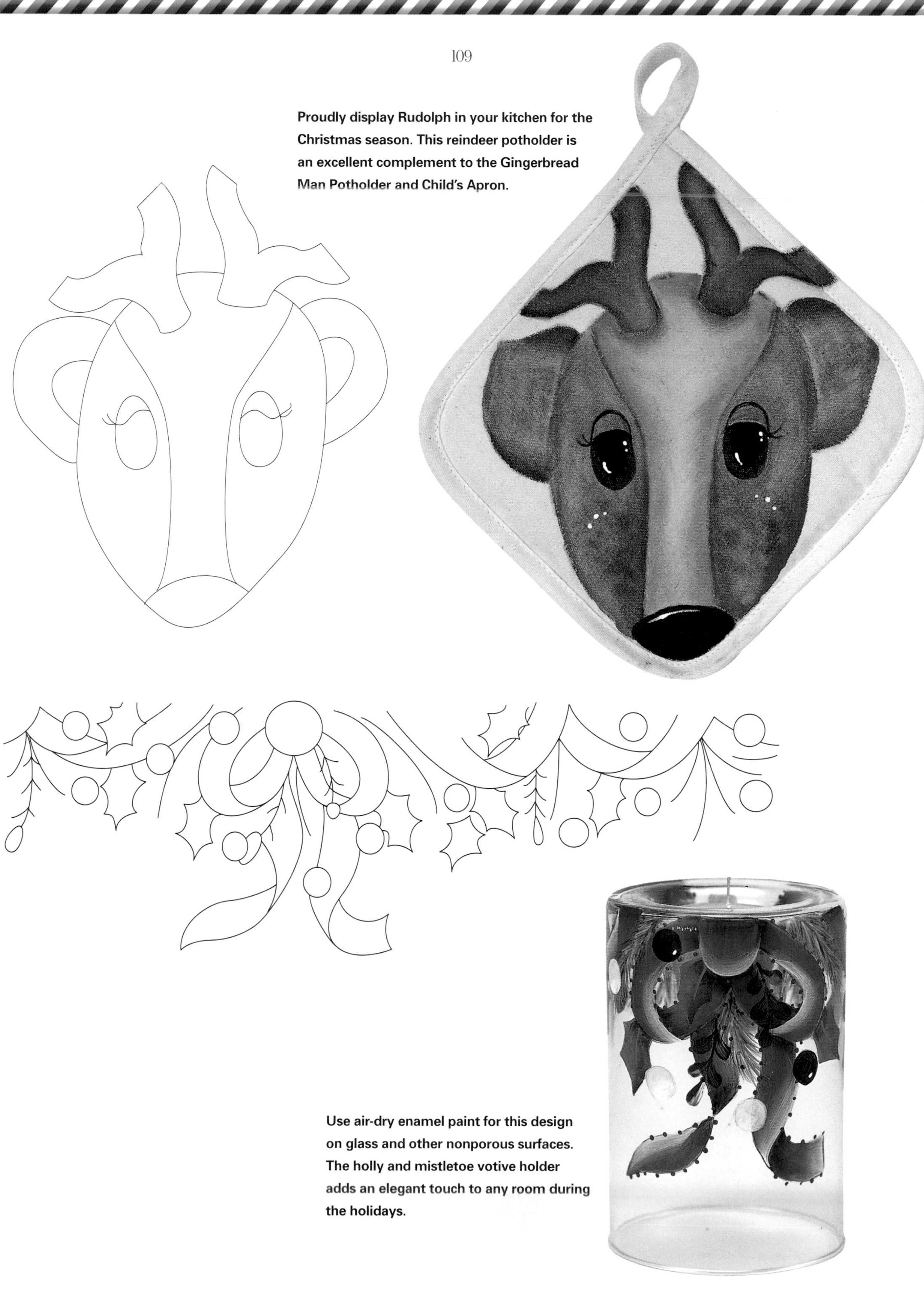

Use air-dry enamel paint for this design on glass and other nonporous surfaces. The holly and mistletoe votive holder adds an elegant touch to any room during the holidays.

RESOURCES

For paint, brushes and other materials, contact the following suppliers:

United States

DecoArt
P.O. Box 327
Stanford, KY 40484
Phone: (606) 365-3193
Fax: (606)365-9739
www.decoart.com
paint@decoart.com

Delta Technical Coatings, Inc.
2550 Pellissier Place
Whittier, CA 90601
Phone: (800) 423-4135
Fax: (562) 695-5157
www.deltacrafts.com

Hobby Lobby
7707 SW Forty-fourth St.
Oklahoma City, OK 73179
Phone: (405) 745-1100
www.hobbylobby.com

JoAnn Fabrics and Crafts
5555 Darrow Rd.
Hudson, OH 44236
www.joanns.com

Loew-Cornell
563 Chestnut Ave.
Teaneck, NJ 07666
Phone: (201) 836-7070
Fax: (201) 836-8110
www.loew-cornell.com

Michaels Stores Inc.
8000 Bent Branch
Irving, TX 75063
Phone: (800) MICHAELS
www.michaels.com

Royal & Langnickel Brush Mfg. Inc.
6707 Broadway
Merrillville, IN 46410
Phone: (219) 660-4170
www.royalbrush.com

International

Art Supplies Direct (Canada)
Phone: (866) ASD-4ART
www.artsuppliesdirect.com

Art Craft
Pool Road
OTLEY
West Yorkshire
UK
L221 1DY
Phone: (01943) 462195
Fax: (01943) 850074
www.artcraft.co.uk
info@artcraft.co.uk

INDEX

a
Aprons, 38-46, 89
Arms, 50, 90

b
Back-to-back float technique, 11
Banner, 82-83
Beards, 22, 24, 35, 36, 81
Berries, 62, 98
Bows, 45, 89
Brushes
- angle, 8, 10, 11
- Bobbi's Blender, 8, 14
- comb, 8
- deerfoot, 8, 14
- fan, 8, 13
- filbert, 8, 12
- flat, 8, 10, 11, 13
- glaze, 8
- liner, 8, 10, 13
- loading, 10, 11, 12
- mop, 14
- round, 8, 13, 14
- sable, 8
- scrubber, 8, 14
- sponge, 8

Brushstrokes, 12-13
- C stroke, 12, 96
- comma stroke, 13
- leaf stroke, 12
- one stroke, 12

Buttons, 45, 89

c
Candle painting, 9, 16, 20-25
Candy, 26-31, 56-63
Checkerboard technique, 15, 25, 46, 98
Christmas Tree Card Holder project, 100-107
Clothesline, 76
Clothing, 90
Cookies, 42
Corner-load float technique, 11, 97

d-e
Dress, 52-53
Earmuffs, 70, 75
Eyebrows, 36
Fabric painting, 9, 16, 38-46, 47
Faces, 22, 23, 24, 35, 36, 45, 47, 51, 80, 89, 97
Frosted glass finish, 9
Fur, 23, 81-82, 94, 96

g
Gifts, 105-106, 108
Gingerbread boy, 89
Gingerbread Boy Ornament project, 64-67
Gingerbread Man Potholder project, 47
Glass painting, 9, 16, 26-37, 109
Glaze
- clear gloss, 9, 31
- Gossamer Winged Angel project, 48-55

h-l
Hair, 35, 52
Hands, 53, 54
Hats, 23, 35, 70, 72
Headband, 74, 75
Hearts, 67
Holly, 25, 62, 89, 109
Joy Tray project, 92-99
Lid of pot, 76
Lights, 105
Little Helper's Apron project, 38-46
Loading brushes, 10, 11, 12

m-o
Mediums
- candle and soap painting, 9, 16
- textile, 9, 16, 41, 47

Metal painting, 9, 17, 84-91
Metal primer, 9
Mistletoe, 109
Mittens, 70, 73-74
Moon, 36
Mustache, 25, 36, 81
Noel Plaque project, 56-63
Ornaments, 64-67, 105, 108

p
Paint
- acrylic, 9
- medium. See Mediums
- PermEnamels, 9, 16, 109

Palette knife, 9, 13
Paper
- graphite, 9
- palette, 9

Peppermint Stick Candy Jar project, 26-31
PermEnamels, 9, 16, 109
Plaid, 34
Pom-pom, 72-73
Potholder project, 47, 109
Preparing surfaces, 16
Presents. See Gifts

r
Recipe card, 45-46
Reindeer, 96-97, 109
Resources, 110
Ribbon, 95, 106
Robe, 81
Rolling pin, 43-44
Reindeer potholder project, 109

s
Sandpaper, 9
Santa Candle project, 20-25
Santa Moon Saucer project, 32-37
Scarf, 70-71
Scrubbing technique, 14
Sea sponge, 9
Sealer, all-purpose, 9
Snow, 76, 87, 90
Snow Day Pot project, 68-77
Snowman, 76
Snowman and Snowlady Tin project, 84-91
Spattering technique, 13, 91, 99
Stars, 35, 37
Stippling technique, 14, 87-88, 95, 97
Stocking, 95
Strokes. See Brushstrokes
Stylus, 9
Surface conditioner for PermEnamels, 9, 16

t
Techniques
- back-to-back float, 11
- checkerboard, 15, 25, 46, 98
- corner-load float, 11, 97
- scrubbing, 14
- spattering, 13, 91, 99
- stippling, 14, 87-88, 95, 97
- wet-on-wet, 41

Textile medium, 9, 16, 41, 47
Thinner diluant, 9
Trees, 87, 100-105, 107
Treetop Santa project, 78-83

v-w
Votive holder, 109
Wash of color, 10
Wet-on-wet technique, 41
Wood painting, 17, 92-99, 103-107
Wreath, 95